Making Management Simple

A practical handbook for
dealing with everyday
management challenges

Second edition

FRANCES KAY, HELEN GUINNESS AND NICOLA STEVENS

howtobooks

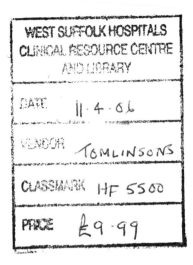
Published by How To Books Ltd,
3 Newtec Place, Magdalen Road,
Oxford OX4 1RE, United Kingdom.
Tel: (01865) 793806. Fax: (01865) 248780.
e-mail: info@howtobooks.co.uk
www.howtobooks.co.uk

© Copyright 2005 Frances Kay, Helen Guinness and Nicola Stevens

British Library Cataloguing in Publication Data.
A catalogue record for this book is available from
the British Library.

First edition 2003
Second edition 2005

Produced for How To Books by Deer Park Productions
Typeset by Kestrel Data, Exeter, Devon
Cover design by Baseline Arts Ltd, Oxford
Printed and bound by Cromwell Press Ltd, Trowbridge, Wiltshire

NOTE: The material contained in this book is set out in good
faith for general guidance and no liability can be accepted
for loss or expense incurred as a result of relying in particular
circumstances on statements made in the book. Laws and
regulations are complex and liable to change, and readers should
check the current position with the relevant authorities before
making personal arrangements.

Contents

Preface

We are excited about this second edition of *Making Management Simple*. Why? Because when we learned about it we realized this proves our theory and the feedback we've received from other people. The problem we found with many management books was that they're full of jargon, buzzwords, hype and theory. For many readers this can be difficult to follow. Their content is often hard to implement, as well as being confusing. Our book offers an alternative: something rather more straightforward, a useful, no-nonsense management handbook in easy to read style.

Don't for one moment imagine that we're saying effective management is easy. It is not, and never will be. On the other hand, in part, the book is simple because it uses common language throughout. We have tried to write about a difficult subject using a strategic approach that emphasises good communication and clarity of purpose. Its aim is to help you, the reader, learn management techniques that promote a sense of inclusion and empowerment at all levels in the workplace.

In this revised edition we have included highlighted tips, points to note and added inspiring quotes to draw the reader's attention to the most important aspects of the topic being discussed. The essence of *Making Management Simple* lies in the *simplicity* of implementing the skills and techniques. It is about a consistent approach and style from the top.

The recurrent feedback on the book shows that highly experienced managers have found it a breath of fresh air and stimulated their leadership ability. It has given them an opportunity to review their management style in the modern business world. For those recent arrivals to managerial status it has been enlightening as they progress into more senior management roles. Organisations have reported to us that it has contributed to a happier corporate culture, better teamwork and improved staff morale.

The problem in my life and other people's lives is not the absence of knowing what to do, but the absence of doing it!

Peter Drucker

We hope you will enjoy this revised edition with its practical approach to meeting management challenges.

Frances Kay, Helen Guinness and Nicola Stevens

Foreword
by Patrick Forsyth

Opening another book about how to manage people might prompt the exclamation '*not ANOTHER one!*' What can one say? Well, quite a bit in this case, as this one is special. I would describe it as an antidote to over-hyped management theory.

Management is easy. It consists of little more than sitting in an ivory tower, issuing instructions and keeping an eye open to see if people need chasing to be sure they are executing them properly. Or so it may seem.

Of course management is, in fact, no easy task and it can prove downright difficult, especially if the overall business or organisational climate in which it is practised is under pressure in any way.

A simple definition will help to set the scene. Management describes the process of achieving results *through* other people – *your people are largely instrumental in your achieving your results.* This is different from your doing things *for* them and it is inherent to the process that management should *add* to what others would otherwise do of their own volition (or there might be considered to be little point in having managers at all).

Managers, of course, often have their own tasks to complete alongside the job of managing others. Yet managing other people is usually crucial; however productive and creative a manager may be, they can never, through their own efforts, make up for ineffective performance amongst their team. Thus the job of being a manager must be carried out effectively if overall results are to be achieved successfully, and this in turn involves many different tasks.

Bob Scholey describes management thus: *'There is no magic in management. I make sure that people know what they are doing and then see that they do it.'* If it still sounds easy, then consider the following anecdote (which is reproduced from *Hook Your Audience*: Management Pocketbooks):

Once upon a time . . . there was a wolf. He was scruffy, bedraggled and generally down at heel. He scratched a living where he could, but was regarded by the other animals as very low in the pecking order. He hated this; he wanted to be well regarded and, after long fruitless hours trying to think how he could change his image, he concluded he needed help. He asked an aardvark, an anteater and an antelope for advice. Nothing: though the antelope suggested that he ask the lion – *after all he's king of the jungle.* Risky it might be, but he was desperate, so he went and – very carefully – approached the lion, saying – *'I want people to like me. I don't want to be thought of as just a scruffy lowlife: I want to be loved. What can I do? Please advise me, your Majesty.'*

The lion was irritated by the interruption, but he paused and gave it a moment's thought – '*You should become a bunny rabbit,*' said the lion. '*Everyone loves a bunny rabbit. I think it's the long floppy ears and the big eyes. Yes, that's it – become a bunny rabbit.*' The wolf did the wolf equivalent of touching his forelock, thanked the lion and slunk away. But almost at once he thought – '*Wait a minute, how do I become a bunny rabbit?*' He went back, risked interrupting the lion again and said – '*Sorry – excuse me, your Majesty. It is, of course, a wonderful idea of yours this business of my becoming a bunny rabbit, but . . . but how, exactly, do I do that?*'

The lion drew himself up to his full height, ruffled his mane and said simply: '*As king of the jungle, I'm concerned with strategy – how you do it is for you to work out.*'

Enough digression, but this is precisely the point I want to make about this book. I would define the phrase 'antidote to over-hyped management theory' I used earlier as having a how-to focus. There is surely sound theory acting as a foundation to what is written here. But there is also a wealth of practical experience that has allowed the distillation of core issues from the mass of possible comment that could be made about the management process. Nothing is over-engineered; there is advice and guidance here aplenty that can really help. The book provides a hands-on blueprint for success as a manager.

If you identify the things that are key, and do the key things right, then not half but most of the battle is won. Management may not in fact be inherently easy, but it is made much simpler, and the unforeseen and dynamic circumstances that it must cope with can be better tamed, if this is done. More importantly, if you achieve this focus then your targeted results will be more likely to be reached by you and your people; and it is results upon which you are doubtless judged.

Patrick Forsyth, Touchstone Training and Consultancy

Patrick Forsyth is a management trainer, consultant and business author. His books, published by How To Books, include: *Appraising Job Performance, Successful Negotiating, Persuasive Business Writing* and *The Management Speaker's Handbook.* He can be contacted on *patrick@touchstonm firstnet.co.uk*

Introduction: Management in the 21st Century

Management (n.) 1 The process or an instance of managing or being managed. 2 (a) the professional administration of business concerns, public undertakings, etc. (b) the people engaged in this. (c) a governing body; a board of directors or the people in charge of running a business, regarded collectively.

MANAGEMENT OVERLOAD

One of the difficulties of management today is that we seem to have too much to do. What do we mean by this? Do we mean limited resources, limited time or too much choice?

This book looks at all aspects of working life and considers management techniques from the biggest companies at the very top through to the sole trader who is trying to make his or her own living. We consider some of the major changes of the 21st century – the fashion for management fads such as re-engineering, downsizing, de-centralising. Diversification was another big thing – going global – do you or don't you?

We will look at how management can impact on working practices today and show that developing relationships, working effectively and producing outstanding results, are not about applying formulae. In fact it's about meeting needs – organisational and individual. Most multi-national companies respect privacy laws which demand that employees are now given private time. Sole traders, on the other hand, feel it does not give them any protection. Nor do many of them believe they can afford to have time out.

Technology should be about giving people permission to carve out the life that suits them and to bring awareness of the best way to get maximum production.

Too much to do?
It is the cry of every busy professional. Yet surely with today's technological advances we should all have more leisure and less onerous work. Where has the 21st century led us to? These changes have given us the ability to do more – hence there is less time in which to do it all. We work faster so there is more work created.

Email is heralded as the wonder post – it goes straight from the source of the letter to the recipient and cuts out the support staff (i.e. no typist, no postage, no paper). But we still print off a hard copy for our files! We still confirm things by a follow-up telephone call or fax.

Good management will always be about improving the bottom line – we can't get away from that. But it needs to be for the good of the staff, as well as the company.

The reality of the modern office

One of the realities of the modern office is that people are beginning to isolate themselves by sending emails to people sitting as close to them as the next desk. Also, writing numerous emails and sending them to 40 unnecessary people is equally heinous. The result is simply huge quantities of junk mail.

People in senior management positions are now wasting vast amounts of time trying to respond to their emails. Sometimes valuable information may be lost simply because people do not have the time to read every single message – especially if its subject matter has not been clearly indicated.

Emails also result in huge work loads for PAs, secretaries and support staff who have to sift through them to find out what their bosses really need to read and what they do not. Very few people truly trust the electronic age, so paper consumption has increased, not decreased.

The myth of the mobile

Consider the huge increase in mobile telephone technology. What has it done for us? People who choose to live out of London find it good to have constant communication available. But is it such a good thing never to be off duty? Who really wants to work 24/7? Is the solution a mobile for personal life and another for business life? But then you have twice the trouble! It can be a male/female thing – men perhaps would have less of a problem leaving the family telephone behind than some women.

People have far greater expectations now – all of which come from technological advances. Instant gratification is now expected in all aspects of life. Current legislation should ensure that organisations do allow their employees to have private time. Despite the legislation, evidence would seem to indicate the very opposite: people become married to their companies and end up living to work rather than working to live.

Limited resources

Demographically our workforce is shrinking; simultaneously companies are working leaner and meaner. Organisational structures have flattened out, which has resulted in a loss of career development and succession planning. There are no more jobs for life, no guarantees of on-going employment.

There are fewer people doing more work. The freelance market has increased but there is the problem of integrating freelances with permanent staff. Interim management is quite common although, again there is the problem of integration.

How do you build relationships quickly and meet individual and organisational needs? There are other issues to consider, such as environmental constraints, EU restrictions, standards, rules and regulations. In addition there is the added pressure of globalisation.

Constant change

The IT revolution calls for constant changes in working methods and patterns. We have moved away from Schumacher's idea of small is beautiful. Mergers and acquisitions are the order of the day – the bigger the better? Perhaps – but also much more unwieldy. It also makes communication and relationship building that much more of a challenge, to say nothing of the business of integrating different organisational cultures.

Materialism and the obsession of being profit driven

We live in a single-minded, materialistic world that has resulted in the obsession with being profit driven. Naturally companies need to make profits but not at the expense of quality of life.

Danger of management fads

As well as information overload, management theories are plentiful, gurus come and go. Management theories can be too prescriptive (therefore inflexible) and often over-complicate and cloud the issues. They tend to deal with the symptoms rather than the cause. So we end up with Band-Aid solutions that may provide temporary change for the better but don't tackle the underlying disease. *Result: the symptoms return.*

The antidote: the necessity for and advantages of making management simple

Making management simple is common sense. It is clear, connected communication. It is non-prescriptive and individuality is acknowledged. It's about making connections, building relationships and being inclusive. It's about creating understanding, being accountable and taking responsibility for the whole, not just for your own area. It's about getting the buy-in and generating personal motivation.

If we practised making management simple, it would free up management practice today. Management in the 21st century is 'joined up' in every sense of the word. The traditional barriers of the differences between the sexes have become eroded. It is simple in the sense that we have the ability to look and see what the framework is. It enables us to think what the overall consequences are on the rest of the company – not just as an entity, but on the individuals within the company who make up that whole.

Working relationships are an intrinsic part of it. Making management simple gives a comprehensive practical framework, from both male and female perspectives.

A cautionary tale . . .

A turkey was chatting with a bull. 'I would love to be able to get to the top of that tree,' sighed the turkey, 'but I haven't got the energy.' 'Well, why don't you nibble on some of my droppings?' replied the bull. 'They're packed with nutrients.' The turkey pecked at a lump of dung and found that it actually gave him enough strength to reach the lowest branch of the tree. The next day, after eating some more dung, he reached the second branch. Finally, after the fourth night, there he was proudly perched at the top of the tree. He was promptly spotted by a farmer, who shot the turkey out of the tree.

Management lesson? Bullshit might get you to the top, but it won't keep you there.

MANAGEMENT MAGIC

Management magic – some things may work for everybody (general principles, boundaries, ground rules) and there are other things that work for individuals. The magic of making management simple is finding the way that suits you and your personal situation. But more importantly, as a manager, it is finding the way that best suits the people with whom you work.

Making management simple is about respecting individual needs and working with them. Even if you work in very different ways, it is essential to find links that enable you to work together. Find suitable times for working together and focus on the things that need to get done. This is more effective than being judgmental or critical about the way other people work or manage. Finding and using the right approach makes all the difference. Each person is unique and will be accustomed to different working situations.

And what if you are a one-man band? Contractual situations with other people require flexibility and understanding. When working with SMEs (small to medium size enter-prises) or large corporations/government agencies/or not for profit organisations – you have to find ways of matching and mirroring the way *they* work rather than imposing the way *you* work. You cannot assume that your way is the right way.

Creating a foundation for success

The difficulties of management in the 21st century are wide-ranging and complex. Be selective of what you do and how you do it. The variety of personalities in the workplace have differing abilities and needs. Foundation for success: just because everyone can do joined-up writing doesn't mean that they are all thinking the same way.

Without going into psychology, there are, for example, other things such as the DISC (dominance, influence, steadiness, compliance) principle that looks at the ways different types of people think and work. If you can find out how someone ticks, it will be an advantage. It makes obvious sense to communicate with others and work with them in a way that they are going to understand.

If you are not on the same wave-length, time is wasted, jobs don't get done. People get frustrated and annoyed. Management fads abound, but they don't always work. They are often prescriptive and do not therefore reflect individual ways of working.

Find a person's unique way and take advantage of it. For instance, use creative people who think outside the box for troubleshooting. Use different ways of communicating – NLP (Neuro-Linguistic Programming) for example.

Dangers

Over-engineering = overcooking? Getting things done is the name of the game. But if you are a perfectionist you may fall into the trap of procrastination. The endless loop of perfection. Perfectionism can produce a fear of finishing – similar to the chaos theory: if you never finish you can't be criticised for being wrong. So – just do it! Time-wasters have perfected the avoidance theory – if the task is not done it is eventually given to someone else. What strategies are available? And what style do you identify with and what suits you?

How getting approaches right makes the difference

By making theory work in practice, by meeting individual and organisational needs, we are making management simple and being flexible to the changeable needs of the individuals and the organisation.

Sir John Harvey-Jones said that every company, no matter how small, must aim to be the best in its market place. The risks of aiming low, he said, are far greater than the risks of aiming high. He believes that people are capable of incredible things if they are given a chance. Good managers ensure that their staff are given that chance. To inspire others, good managers are willing to stand out even when they would prefer to merge with the crowd.

The professional manager knows that by 'giving' they also receive their own reward. They feel better when they solve a challenging problem. They feel proud when the deal they have worked so hard to achieve finally pays off. If managers love what they do, the challenges become the rewards.

FOCUSING ON KEY ISSUES

This book outlines a sound basis for quality and effective management through agreement and performance. It shows how making management simple achieves results. It measures strategies for ensuring a good working relationship at all levels and stages of the management process. A manager's role is to inspire staff to do their best and to create and maintain a workplace that allows them to carry out their work effectively and responsibly.

Successful and effective management can be construed as 'partnering with staff'. This partnership, if successful, produces effective performance, improved productivity and confidence in the workplace in addition to reliability in the services provided within the company.

Managers today don't have to be tough. In the past managers ruled supreme but to get the most from staff now means treating them correctly and with respect. In the succeeding chapters we will be looking at ways to help you through the management maze.

Objectives

Good management is about 'making it work', dealing with things in a simple, not complex, way having confidence, knowing what is right. Enjoying trust and commitment with staff, by way of shared assumptions, shared goals, non-confrontational attitudes and incentives to achievement.

Making management work involves sharing knowledge of the company's objectives, business and culture through organisational linkage – information, processes and team building.

Keys to success are:

◆ Clear vision – past, present and future.

◆ Open communications – internally between management and staff.

◆ Right mix of people.

◆ Commitment – total – from top to bottom and back.

◆ Rewards – creative, reflect performance and motivate at all levels.

The 'ideal' manager as a concept has been researched from time to time. One definition is 'working for someone I learn from'. Managers should always help build strengths and develop potential.

Successful managers understand which elements help achieve performance targets and goals. For example: the right people (experience, qualifications and training); the right approach (attitude, people skills, punctuality, diligence).

What needs to be borne in mind throughout this book is that the process of managing is essentially simple. To quote Patrick Forsyth, author of *Communicating with Your Staff* (Orion Business Books):

> Management is not something you do in a vacuum but is an interaction with other people. Both parties' feelings and attitudes are important, and it is for the manager to take the initiative in creating a way of working that allows for this fact, and equally important, is seen to do so.

This perspective is certainly kept in mind throughout the following chapters. So let's start the process of 'Making Management Simple'.

But first, some ethical questions:

◆ If a bus station is where a bus stops, and a train station is where a train stops, why do they call desks work stations?

◆ If quitters never win, and winners never quit, what fool came up with 'Quit while you're ahead?'

◆ If Fed Ex and UPS were to merge, would they call it Fed Up?

◆ If it's true that we are here to help others, then what exactly are the *others* here for?

◆ How come you don't ever hear about 'gruntled' employees? And who has been dissing them anyhow?

Finally:

◆ If you can't be kind to those with whom you work, at least have the decency to be vague.

1

Getting and Keeping Yourself Organised

Good management is about *achievement*. It demands a productive approach, one that enhances performance, improves situations and adds value. The words that spring to mind are all positive sounding: 'efficient', 'effective', 'develop', 'optimise'.

> *'Tomorrow is always the busiest day of the week.'*
>
> Jonathan Lazair

Whoever you are, whatever you do, as a manager you are no doubt charged with achieving particular things. To achieve anything you have to be organised, and in the hectic and dynamic business world today you must be especially prepared.

TIP

As a manager, you need to make sure that your staff are well organised. There is nothing better than leading by example.

PRODUCTIVITY

It is a simple fact: those who are best organised give themselves a head start in everything that they do. Productivity, effectiveness, hitting targets – all are improved by good strategy, preparation and planning. Anything less hinders achievement, and promotes a view of the manager as a headless chicken, led by events rather than directing their own destiny.

What type of manager are you?

Managers who are qualified accountants know the cost of everything but the value of nothing.

Bankers turned managers lend you an umbrella when the sun is shining but want it back the minute it begins to rain (Mark Twain).

Managers who are ex-economists know tomorrow why the things they predicted yesterday didn't happen today.

A manager with the mind of a mathematician is like a blind man in a dark room looking for a black cat that isn't there.

A manager who is a computer programmer will solve problems for you, which you didn't know you had, in a way you don't understand.

A manager who has studied psychology watches everyone else when a beautiful woman enters the room.

A manager with diplomatic experience will tell you to go to hell in such a way that you will look forward to the trip.

The best managers work actively at *maximising efficiency* and *creating opportunities* to improve situations throughout their sphere of influence.

Good managers constantly keep their eyes above the desk and spend time generating policies, procedures, systems and routines which save time and prevent crises and problems arising in future.

Managers who are trouble-shooters are at best simply fire-fighting. That is a *reactive*, not *proactive*, function. The words that best describe them are 'maintain', 'ensure' and 'prevent'. If at the end of the day the situation at work is slightly better than it was at the beginning, the trouble-shooter manager believes they have been successful. This is a non-productive, survival role. These people have little time to consider longer-term issues.

TIME MANAGEMENT

Does managing your time really matter? Is it important? *Yes!* Without an ability to manage time, you will not be an effective manager; less is achieved and productivity falls. Time can be managed – if you don't believe this, stop reading right now! If you doubt what we're saying, consider the words *time control*, if that is easier. Controlling time means better handling of the elements of surprise which erode everyone's working day. If steps are taken to avoid interruptions, productivity and achievement immediately rise. There is no magic formula here, to a degree success is in

Exercise 1

Find out what kind of manager you are:

Ask five people what they think of your management skills. (*This is 360° feedback made simpler.*)

A manager was called into the boardroom halfway through a directors' meeting. She waited while two of her senior company directors finished their discussion. They were describing an individual in glowing terms, depicting personal qualities and attributes. When they had finished the manager asked if there was any chance of headhunting this paragon as it seemed the company would benefit from these many abilities. 'No need,' said one of the directors, 'she already works here. We were discussing you!'

Provided you ask people whose opinion you respect and who will give an honest, unsycophantic answer, you may be agreeably surprised at their perception of your management skills.

Exercise 2

To work out whether you are 'productive' or a 'fire-fighter' ask yourself these five questions:

1. When planning your day, do you choose:
   a) the routine tasks
   b) the difficult jobs
   c) the unpleasant jobs
   d) the creative jobs?
2. Do you use a 'to-do' list for each day?
3. If so, what kind of jobs are left unfinished at the end of the day?
4. Are you aware of Parkinson's Law – 'Work expands to fill the time available'?
5. Do you know when your mind is most productive and do you plan to do the most exacting jobs at that time of day?

If you have answered (A) or (D) to question 1, and have answered No to two other questions, you need to read to the end of this chapter!

the details and the effect is cumulative. *Everything you do, every constructive habit you develop*, can help improve your situation.

Mark Forster, author of *Get Everything Done and Still Have Time to Play* says 'you can't manage your time well unless you know what you want to achieve.' But in order to do that, it helps to know *yourself.*

We are all different – some people function effectively well into the evening yet cannot cope with a dawn start. What type of person are you, and when are the peaks and troughs of your day?

The early riser: Some of us wake up at 7 am (or even earlier) raring to go. If you are not in this category, avoid arranging breakfast meetings! You need a later time in order to be effective. One thing that can help you to wake up is sunlight. It is a natural alarm call and the more you can soak up the livelier you will feel.

Reluctant Risers: If you find mornings difficult have a simple but nutritious breakfast. Cereals like bran flakes or oats are high in fibre. They are slow energy releasers and with some fruit as well your blood sugar (and also your energy) levels will be maintained.

Travellers: On the way to work do a crossword. It not only reduces stress but research shows that regularly exercising the brain with puzzles helps prevent memory loss and guards against brain diseases.

Planners: Get out your daily task sheet – list in order of 1 to 10 or rank them like celebrities – A or B. Isolate the three most important tasks and complete them first thing. Ticking them off once they have been totally completed will make you feel really good.

Brainy types: When you have blinding ideas and brain power surges make sure you have paper with you to write things down. You may not always be at your desk when this happens – recent research has shown that women are likely to have their most creative thoughts when talking to friends and men have flashes of inspiration when sitting on the loo!

Lunchers: Try to avoid huge meals. If possible choose a light lunch or a healthy snack and take some exercise to avoid the afternoon slump. Walking and breathing deeply helps you to stay calm and relax.

PM blues: To help avoid this energy low-point make sure your posture is correct and have regular drinks of water. Do some exercises at the desk to avoid RSI. Take a walk around the office – have a caffeine break.

Late Taskers: At the end of the day make the next day's work easier by listing the tasks you will tackle first thing in the morning. If you can find time to fit in a workout at the gym on the way home you will go home feeling great. If not, try to find time for a swim. Alternatively take a brisk walk home and avoid the crowded buses and tubes.

Now that we've looked at what type of people there are, the next step is to get organised.

NOTE

Remember, it's not the *hours* you work that are important, it's what you do *during those hours* that matters.

Recent survey results show that many senior managers today would like to control or reduce the amount of time they spend working. If you are going to succeed in being productive, certainly if you are to achieve a satisfactory work/life balance, you need to monitor your current situation.

Exercise 3

Question your current practice by asking yourself the following questions. Do you:

◆ reguarly spend longer than ten hours working per day?

◆ need to take work home three or more times per week?

◆ find yourself dreaming about your job?

◆ have sleepless nights because of work pressures?

◆ cancel holidays or weekend plans because of work?

If you have answered Yes to three or more of the above, here's how to improve the situation.

The key is being able to achieve results *without* working hope lessly long hours. If you are seen to be effective, then you are perceived as efficient.

But be aware of the rules of the work place, for instance:

♦ A tidy desk may indicate an efficient person, but to some bosses an empty in-tray indicates an empty mind.

♦ If the company has a 'presenteeism' culture, it may not be wise to be seen leaving your work place on time every day.

♦ To be effective and do a good job, develop habits that don't conflict with ideas held by key players in your organisation.

♦ Create a reputation for adding value by improving performance/morale of your group/department.

♦ Learn how to manage change positively and productively to achieve good results (see Chapter 7).

Your time should be organised in such a way that, overall, you are focused in your activity on what is most important. Everything about your approach must assist in prompting good productivity.

There are many ways, these include:

- Spend more time on planning and thinking. For example, look at everything you have to do for the day/week/ month. If you spend time prioritising your week, you need only spend a few minutes prioritising your day.

- Make sure you assess what is urgent and deal with it first.

- Chunking: get your tasks sorted – print out emails, dig out letters and faxes, list them all on a piece of paper, then sort them into piles relating to each task – write/ meet/phone/delegate.

- Set aside some time each day for interacting with staff and colleagues – but do have a time limit and stick to it.

- Actively delegate tasks and responsibilities to members of your department and set achieveable deadlines for them to cope with.

- Aim to complete three tasks off your 'daily task list'.

- Plan time to relax/take time out.

What makes all this possible is simple – it is *you*! You must create your own destiny in terms of time and productivity.

It helps to think things through, develop a focus on individual elements, and to categorise the task in some way.

NOTE

There are four key areas that require a manager's time:

◆ **Routine communications:** paperwork, admin, exchanging information.

◆ **Traditional role:** planning, controlling, decision-making.

◆ **People management:** motivation, conflict resolution, discipline, training and development.

◆ **Business Development:** necessary to increasing profile by interacting with others both in and out of the company.

With this sort of manageable picture in mind you will find it easier to take concrete steps to organise yourself. How exactly? You need a *plan*.

Action plan

Decide how much time you are going to devote to each of the above categories each day/week and create your own time management activity sheet. Block out the times with the appropriate task and amount of time required. (Suggested example below or incorporate this in your daily planner/electronic diary.)

Ideally the day should be divided into chunks to reflect the various demands of the role. (For the purposes of this illustration, we have labelled the four types of managerial tasks A, B, C and D. This does not reflect their order of priority.)

- Routine communications   **A** tasks
- Traditional role   **B** tasks
- People management   **C** tasks
- Business/Client Development   **D** tasks

Managerial Time Activity Sheet		
Day		Week commencing . . . .
Before 9am	A tasks	(paperwork)
	D tasks	(networking breakfasts)
9am	C tasks	(staff meetings)
10am	B tasks	(planning, decision-making)
11am	B tasks	(planning, decision-making)
12noon	D tasks	(reception)
1pm	D tasks	(Client lunch meeting)
2pm	C tasks	(Staff interview/appraisal)
3pm	A tasks	(Admin/exchange information)
4pm	B tasks	(planning)
5pm	A tasks	(paperwork)
6pm and after	D tasks	(Presentation)

Suggested example:

Managerial Time Activity Sheet		
Day: Tuesday		Week commencing 4 February 200x
07.00	A task	Train to Bristol (reading/admin)
07.45	D task	Chamber of Commerce business breakfast
09.15	A task	Return train journey (reading/ report)
10.00	C task	Departmental meeting – staff appraisals
11.30	B task	Deskwork – forecast for 200x/200x
12.00	D task	Partners' meeting – pre-lunch reception
12.45	D task	Williams Seymour – client lunch
14.30	C task	Interview – assistant manager replacement
15.30	A task	PA – delegation of weekly admin
16.00	B task	Presentation for client meeting (final check)
17.30	A task	Preparation for Wednesday
18.30–20.00	D task	South West Regional presentation

Planning

There is an old maxim that tells us to *plan the work and work the plan.* You not only need a plan, you need to develop a method for smart working: **S–M–A–R–T**.

◆ **Set task times:** Divide your day/week into sections. If on Mondays you want to be at your desk – avoid meetings that take you out of your office. If you like Fridays to catch up with end of week tasks – block out the time to do this.

◆ **Make goals:** Clearly defined objectives help focus the mind and keep you motivated. Avoid setting yourself unachievable deadlines.

◆ **Ask for help:** Never muddle through. Delegate anything you can. Enlist expertise of others whose skills complement your own.

◆ **Reflect:** Rather than react. Avoid committing to anything until you have all the facts – a hasty decision could lead to unnecessary stress.

◆ **Think – use your brain:** Never be afraid to leave a task if you are stumped. Like exam techniques, if you don't dwell on it but switch to another task, by the time you return to the problem your subconscious may well have a solution!

Staying 'on plan'

Patrick Forsyth, who writes on management techniques, is the author of *First Things First* which deals with time management. His advice on keeping to a time management plan is as follows.

There are two main influences that combine to keep you from completing planned tasks. These are *other people and events*, and *you*.

Let us start with *You*. You may, for example, put off things because you are:

◆ unsure of what to do

◆ dislike the task

◆ prefer another task (despite the clear priority)

◆ fear the consequences.

Time can also be wasted in the reverse way. What tasks do you spend too long on (or resist delegating) because you *like* them? Be honest! Often this is a major cause of wasted time, as is flattering yourself that no one else can do something as well as you can. (Perhaps you do not delegate in case they prove *more able* than you at it! It is a thought worth pondering.) Such things may be one off or, worse in their potential for wasting time, regular.

Certainly there are principles to be noted in this area: a main one is the fallacy that things get easier if left. Virtually always the reverse is true. Faced with sacking a member of staff, to take a dramatic example, many people will constantly prevaricate. They may want to 'see how things go', 'check the end of month results' or some such, when swift action (all the checks in fact having been done) is best all round.

The second area of problems that keep you from the key tasks are the classic interruptions. We all have some colleagues who, when they stick their heads round the door and say, 'Have you got a minute?' mean half an hour minimum is about to vanish unconstructively. Saying 'no' is an inherent part of good time management.

Telephones can be the bane of our lives. Voicemail in its many forms can dilute any client relationship, so use sparingly! There are moments when it is necessary to be unavailable – some tasks can be completed in a quiet hour, yet take much longer if we are constantly interrupted. This applies especially to anything that requires some real thought or creativity.

There are many ways of avoiding interruptions, these include:

◆ If the telephone rings constantly – switch on the voice-mail option for two hours.

◆ Set boundaries about when to check emails – suggest twice a day.

◆ Make use of cancellations by having some 'fill-in' tasks ready to tackle.

◆ Ensure that meetings have a short agenda and set a time limit.

◆ If you work in an office which has a door – close it at certain times. This will cut down on casual interruptions. Only those with important queries will try to gain entry and, hopefully, most of them will probably have the courtesy to knock first!

To be able to plan you must know, with some certainty, what your priorities are and organise accordingly. To achieve more you will find it easier if, for the most part, you do *one* thing at a time.

Prioritising

The ability to *prioritise* is essential.

TIP

One chief executive had to decide which were the most important tasks for him to tackle. Each day he made a list of things he wanted to get done. He divided his list into categories A and B. He tore the list in half. He put the B list into the waste bin and kept the A list. He then divided the A list into A and B categories and repeated the process. After three attempts he arrived at the matters most urgently requiring his attention and dealt with them straight away.

This might not suit everyone (though do try it!), but you do need to approach things in a systematic way.

NOTE

The ability to prioritise is what all successful people are able to do. Successful people develop the habit of doing things they *don't like*.

If you can work out the important from the unimportant, you will feel more in control and work more efficiently. Important things require quality time. Urgent things have to be done quickly otherwise problems will result.

The following quadrant shows graphically four overall categories into which tasks can be put.

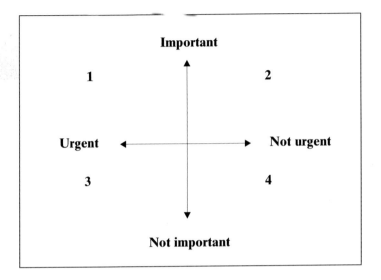

Assign each of your tasks to one of the quadrants. Then:

◆ If something is both urgent and important – put it to the top of your A list.

◆ Deal with the urgent jobs first but deal with them quickly. They are the firefighting, crisis management things.

◆ Spend as much time as possible on 'important' and 'not urgent' tasks as they are the ones that will have the most impact on your business.

◆ Most of the things in the 'not urgent' and 'not important' quadrant are best outsourced or ignored.

The well organised manager:

◆ Makes the most of their personal strengths – *use them.*

◆ Takes advantage of technology – *let the machines take the strain, where appropriate.*

◆ Is punctual and uses time gaps productively for fill-in tasks.

◆ Takes regular breaks – *schedule coffee, lunch and tea breaks to make sure you unwind, relax and replenish.*

◆ Clears their desk – *dump junk* (papers, emails and para-phernalia).

A young assistant at an early stage in his career, was asked by his senior manager to attend a meeting which was being held in conference room C at 9.30am. When he arrived he found the door was locked. He tried to enter, but could not gain admittance. He asked several people whether the meeting had been relocated but no one knew anything about it. Some time later he saw his boss and explained that he had been unable to attend as he could not find the meeting. He was told that the meeting had taken place, in Conference Room C at 9.30am. The young man assured the manager that he had tried to get in. His manager advised him that the procedure in his department was to lock the door at the allotted starting time. The assistant was never late again.

> ## TIP
>
> Every aspect of your work can be made more effective if you organise yourself and your time. It may need some thought. It may well be difficult. But one thing is for sure, getting to grips with this area helps make your overall management role simpler.

Avoiding workaholism

Being busy is not the same as being effective. And being over-busy, and either liking it or persuading yourself that there is no other way, defines being a workaholic. This is harmful to everyone. It is an addiction and leads to a vicious circle in which:

◆ Workaholics find it impossible to say No whatever the circumstances and however impossible it is to achieve the objectives or the deadline.

◆ They also avoid accepting offers of help.

◆ They are poor delegators and fear that by sub-contracting, the job will be less well done.

◆ They develop a reputation for getting things done, so even more work is heaped upon them.

◆ Because they pay such little attention to training and development of their staff, these individuals are de-motivated and frustrated and staff turnover for the workaholic senior manager is high.

There are elements here that are picked up elsewhere (see Chapter 4 – Delegation – and Chapter 5.

TEN AIDS TO REDUCING STRESS

To end this chapter here are some final ideas. They range wide, but then that is exactly what you need to do to maximise effectiveness in this area.

◆ Laughter is a great stress buster. Spend time with optimistic people.

◆ If something has gone wrong don't take it personally. Leave it and move on. Be flexible – best laid plans don't always work out.

◆ Avoid external stimulants – coffee, alcohol or tobacco.

◆ Breathing – take some deep breaths and have some exercise during the day.

◆ Relax in a bath when you get home.

◆ Have a duvet day – become a hermit!

◆ Take up a new hobby.

◆ Stroke a pet (if you have one)!

◆ Focus on a treat – your forthcoming holiday or weekend away.

◆ Be thankful you're not Japanese – they actually have a word which means death from overwork – *karoshi*!

SUMMARY

Good time management is a real asset to anyone's productivity and effectiveness. It is worth exploring the possibilities, instilling the right habits and avoiding any dilution of your firm intentions. And results increase in a firm where everyone is similarly motivated. So how to summarise? *Brrr, Brrr* – excuse me, the telephone is ringing.

2

Being Effective

No manager ever strives to be ineffective – but how is it that some managers are considered effective and command respect and loyalty, and others do not? Being an effective manager is not just about being organised, getting your team to hit sales targets and within budget – even if those are the elements of a manager's work on which they are praised. An effective manager is someone who is totally engaged in the process of managing without blurring the lines of responsibility, relationship and accountability between themselves and others. They need to keep the broader picture in mind and foster the best possible environment for employees to excel in their work.

You have to learn to treat people like a resource . . . you have to ask not what do they cost, but what is the yield, what can they produce?

Peter Drucker

For some managers this comes easily. They have natural charisma and style people look up to. But, for others, however competent they are in their professional expertise, they do not command respect, loyalty and trust easily. They need to develop their own natural communication style and workplace relationships. This is a vital dynamic for any manager, which brings together their professional skills, talents and experience to lead the way. Being effective is based on the willingness to keep an open mind, learn from others, be ready to accept responsibilities and be accountable for actions.

During a recent qualitative attitude survey in a group of UK companies (Nicola Stevens and Associates), the staff and managers across the board were asked what made their own 'boss' effective. They came up with the following conclusions:

◆ They required loyalty and trust in them as individuals and as a group.

◆ The boss needed to be decisive and have a clear sense of direction they could understand.

◆ They valued being managed in a consistent manner – this greatly reduced the stresses and strains when everyone knew what to expect – plus active support and development personally and professionally.

◆ All the members appreciated being able to learn from the manager, but in turn valued the willingness on the part of the manager to ask others in the team for their opinions and expertise.

◆ They wanted to be respected and to respect as a two-way action. As one of the team put it, 'Don't penalise, no false praise, don't blame. Be inspiring'.

In this chapter, to be an effective manger we will review:

◆ Defining your job – and its role.

◆ Assembling resources and forging necessary relations.

◆ Focusing on the job in hand and the results.

◆ Seeing the broader picture.

◆ Decision-making – the buck stops here.

◆ Problem-solving – taking the drama out of a crisis.

DEFINING YOUR JOB AND ITS ROLE

It may seem too obvious to mention – but do you know what your job as a manager requires of you, and its role in the work place?

Many managers, on reflection, discover they are not truly clear about their role and the best possible way to go about it. Often they are horrified to discover that in spite of all their hard work, the long hours are seen as a lack of effectiveness, rather then their efforts to get to grips and keep on top of the job.

Case history

With a move to increase revenue, a media organisation decided to restructure the internal use of specialist equipment and offer it for hire externally. The manager put in charge of this new project had the responsibility of the cross company coordination. After six months of running the project, the main impression he gave others was that he was always seen flitting around from one department and team to another being very 'busy', while they got on with the 'real' work. As a result he was nicknamed 'the butterfly'. His own team's 'in' joke was that if anyone needed to speak to him, they should never to try to find him, but stand still, and sooner or later he would flap past them. They certainly knew what to expect from their manager, but he was seen in a negative light.

The manager knew he was working long hours, trying to build up this new project, doing the best he could. When he took over the project he was aware that there would be new working practices and systems needed that would challenge long-serving employees.

In many ways the project was achieving its aims and could be considered a possible success to be translated through other parts of the organisation. However, one of the board directors saw the problematic way the manager seemed to working and the stress it appeared to cause him and his team.

Almost all quality improvement comes via simplification of design, manufacturing layout, processes and procedures.

Tom Peters

Doing a quick, informal feedback through the team and departments affected by the new project, the director was saddened to hear that the manager's current reputation was summed up in the negative words, listed overleaf under ineffective behaviour, when he knew the manager to encompass all the positive and effective behaviours in the past. That was why he had been given the promotion in the first place.

Negative – ineffective behaviour		Positive – effective behaviour
Evasive	**E**	Encouragement
Falter	**F**	Forward-thinking
Frustration	**F**	Fun
Enigma	**E**	Experience
Callous	**C**	Confidence
Troublesome	**T**	Trust
Insincere	**I**	Inspiring
Visionless	**V**	Vision and values
Ego	**E**	Effective

Negative – uninspiring behaviour		Positive – inspiring behaviour
Ineffective	**I**	Initiative
Nervous	**N**	Natural
Suffering	**S**	Serene
Pressured	**P**	Punctual
Insincere	**I**	Impressive
Rigid	**R**	Relaxed
Embarrassed	**E**	Effective

A meeting resulted in the director realising that there were some gaps in management responsibility within the company. With so many new possibilities and ways of going about the project, there had been no chances of reflection and feedback for the manager to assess the tasks in hand.

The manager had proved himself to be both effective and inspiring in the past in different roles. Having found their new manager ineffective, this team described his actions and contact with them as ineffective and uninspiring.

Consider the words connected to EFFECTIVE and INSPIRE in the two sets of columns above.

If anyone at work was to give you a mark in your use of these action words – good and bad (left-hand and right-hand columns) – how do you think you would be marked? What do those around you, who work with and for you, think about your *modus operandi* in the work place?

Questions – 360 degree feedback
Two simple, but important, direct questions to ask for informal 360 degree managerial feedback:

◆ Do my team know what I want from them?

◆ Do I know what my team want from me?

Action

◆ Now ask the team and other managers for their opinion.

Analysis

◆ Areas of development from feedback.

◆ What insights has that given you?

◆ What were the surprises, good, bad, ugly and interesting?

◆ Where do you need to improve?

Action plan

Draw up lists under:

(1) Talents and skills
(2) Areas I am most appreciated in
(3) Areas I need to freshen up
(4) Skills I need to learn.

Through the kind of analysis shown above the result of the case history was that the director realised that the board had been ineffective in arranging ongoing support and opportunities for the manager, especially as his direct report was unable to give the necessary backing and encouragement. This had a negative effect on the manager and was a knock on his team. All parties concerned at all levels got together to work out the best way forward. They reviewed the progress to date, established what worked and built on those elements, while letting go of unproductive behaviour. Everyone's role was defined within the project and a system of support and cooperation was set up.

TIP

Often company culture completely ignores the fact that the process of effective management includes managing upwards as well as downwards.

Assembling resources and forging necessary relationships

Effective management encompasses the two-way process of managing upwards and downwards. To do this effectively means assembling resources and forging necessary relationships.

*'Leadership is about creating an **alignment of strengths** and making people's weaknesses irrelevant.'*

Peter Drucker

It does not matter whether you are a first time or experienced manager or the head of the company, sooner or later you will need to assemble the resources needed and forge the necessary relationships to be able to do the job.

Questions

◆ How do I like to be managed?

◆ What do I need to be able to do my job?

◆ What support do I need to ask for?

◆ Do I take the time to 'walk the floor' and informally touch base throughout the organisation?

Action

◆ Ask all those involved what support they would like from their manager to enable them to perform at their best.

Action plan

◆ What resources do you need to be able to achieve these requests?

◆ What are the necessary relationships that are needed to achieve this?

Returning to the case history, it was recommended that they establish and develop three new managerial practices:

(1) **Sponsorship.**
(2) **Mentoring and reverse mentoring programme.**
(3) **Empowerment and participation.**

Sponsorship
Sponsorship is a means to engage a senior member of the company to champion existing interests of departments and new projects. All too often the manager is left to 'get on with the job'. Remember 'Don't ask me how – just do it' from the Foreword. In one sense it can be seen as empowering to the manager. But all too often, if unseen problems and issues arise, there is a need to be able to weigh up the options available and the consequences in light of the broader picture.

NOTE

If there is an issue that challenges the policies of the company, or presents new opportunities, then the decision to go ahead or not, probably lies at boardroom level, or with the stakeholders of the business.

Case History
A project sponsor can also take the role of 'manager of loose ends'. In the case of one company, the technology department was responsible for the customising, installing and tutoring of a new accounting package. Once the software was up and running, questions arose as to who was responsible for the day-to-day running of the software. The department went back to their sponsor and agreed it was a waste of their resources to continue with the routine running

of the software, but until the issue of responsibility was resolved the sponsor would oversee the options available within the company, and so 'manage the loose ends' of the project. Later it was agreed to transfer the day-to-day running of the package to the HR department, which the sponsor oversaw.

Mentoring and reverse mentoring programme
A mentor is a person with a depth of industry related ex-perience who is willing to impart their knowledge and support others in their development and growth within the industry. Rather like the sponsor, a mentor is supportive, but has the added advantage of forming a long-term relation-ship with the mentee to aid them in areas of professional development as they present themselves. This is usually an informal relationship, but it creates a readily available opportunity to discuss business concerns, personal career aspirations and networking prospects.

Reverse mentoring is a recent concept. It acknowledges the growth of new technology industries and the business opportunities of implementing these into traditional sectors. In order to realise the full benefits available to more ex-perienced managers, it is more likely that younger members of staff understand the working and possibilities of the new technology. Reversing the mentoring process, from wisdom to inexperience around to expertise to experience, opens up innovative business opportunities and benefits which were previously inconceivable.

> **TIP**
>
> A policy of participate and empowerment fosters a culture of trust, understanding and respect.

Empowerment and participation

To manage effectively means maximising all resources available. It is extremely important that managers aim to develop employees to their full potential. Empowered members of a team provide true value to the organisation. They have the abilities to fully participate and influence the outcome of the manager's decisions and actions. They can provide input to management as decisions are being made, and know that their contribution is valued whether or not it is acted upon in the final analysis. This shows that there is a trust, understanding and respect between both parties. This is particularly important on occasions, when the manager may not be able to reveal the broader picture owing to business sensitive information.

An effective manager works with employees knowing they are a power base in their own right, through the value of their knowledge and perspective. Such a manager takes the time and effort to build relationships at all levels throughout the whole organisation to achieve excellence for the business, their team and themself.

FOCUSING ON THE JOB IN HAND AND RESULTS

Evolution, assessment and refinement

Managing effectively meaning focusing on the job and

getting the results needed. Along the way there needs to be the ability and time to assess, stay on track or recalibrate to get the project back on line. On some occasions, however good the theory seemed in those early meetings, it does not quite work. Then it's back to the drawing board. Turning theory into practice is a skill. The effective manager knows there needs to be a point of aim and action plan to work with that factors in time for evolution, assessment and refinement.

To do this in the most effective way, the manager and team need to be focused and working with purpose.

Doing it with purpose
Classify yourself and your team according to the groupings below.

◆ High focus, low energy = **disengaged**.

◆ Low focus, low energy = **procrastinating**.

◆ High energy, low focus = **distracted**.

◆ High energy, high focus = **purpose – results**.

Heike Bruch and Sumantra Ghosal studied managers for *Harvard Business Review* and found that on average 10% of managers were purposeful compared to 40% distracted, 20% disengaged and 30% procrastinating (reported in *Management Today*, May 2002).

It is disturbing reading to see that it is possible on average to have 50% of any team with low energy. That means only a half of the total team is interested with high energy – but it is really alarming to see these results showing only 10% with high focus are going to achieve the results with professionalism. No one likes to have to 'carry people', but if you follow these ratings, then 90% of your team are not engaged and giving you a full day's work for a full day's pay. Those adrenaline fuelled, high energy people are as unproductive as the low energy, disengaged groups.

TIP

Focus and purpose helps sustain excellence in the work place.

Focus is not recognised as a professional skill. It is rarely practised in a way to sustain excellence. However, the positive use of focus is essential in order to obtain results and sustain productivity.

Questions

◆ Where are you on the purpose groupings?

◆ Where are the members of your team?

Being able to perform 100% in the work place, and sustain that level, means a manager needs to be able to self-manage and inspire that principle in those around them. They need to expect others to give 100% of themselves, showing by example that they also give the full 100% of themselves to the job. This does not mean being in the office for long hours, working over the weekends, being too busy to take holidays and rushing around like the manager nicknamed 'the butterfly'. To sustain the 'high energy, high focus' frame, the manager needs to define ways to use their and their team's energy effectively within the working day, while still leading a balanced life outside the office hours.

Often he who does too much, does too little.

Anon

Analysis of matrix results

◆ What do you need to do to move everyone into the high energy, high focus box?

◆ What do you need to do to sustain that purposeful professional behaviour?

Analysis routines

The everyday activities of emails, meetings and client visits need to be scheduled in on a regular, but defined, basis. For example, download and reply to emails only twice a day, morning and afternoon. Only have a meeting with good reason. Have regular team meetings where everyone knows what is expected of them in advance to prepare. This saves wasted time looking embarrassed and humming or hawing while a new date is arranged because information is missing. Make sure these meetings do not became social gatherings, but productive professionally-run meetings. Some managers mark out regular client-only days for meetings and networking. Others have a policy of being able to work at home in peace and quiet if it is for the benefit of the company, for example in the case of writing lengthy reports or reviewing contracts, which demand concentration. Usually on these occasions the manager is contactable by the office if needed urgently. Above all, the time scheduled in for reflection is essential. The most helpful piece of advice a new manager was given was: 'the first 20 minutes of each day are the most important you have – review what you need to do over the next eight hours and plan accordingly.' The same manager was also told that he only needed to work during those eight hours if he worked effectively.

Measurement of purpose

◆ What will the team look like when working together if they move into the high energy, high focus box?

Action plan

◆ What resources do you need to achieve this?

◆ What support do you need to achieve this?

Seeing the broader picture

An effective manager needs to know how to amalgamate the ongoing successful running of business in the present, and bring about new business opportunities using the experience and knowledge of the present and the past. That means that while being present and in overall charge of the daily running of the company, they need to hold in their mind the broader picture of cross-company objectives and future business aspirations.

Sharing knowledge

While the manager is responsible for the overall day-to-day running of business, it is not their job to be swamped by the detail. It is important that they empower their team to do that for them, and build the necessary relationships and rapport with the experts within their sphere to advise them when needed.

In order to ensure the broader picture is kept in the mind of the effective manager, they need to ask the following questions

(1) Do the managers spend enough time focused on the future?
(2) How are priorities for the future decided?
(3) How is the departmental knowledge within the organisation distributed to gain a full perspective of opportunities?
(4) Who takes responsibility for this and sponsors the process?

TIP

Effective mangers communicate regularly with all levels of the organisation.

Effective managers
Effective managers network and collaborate internally and externally. They are seen regularly 'walking the floor' through all departments and touching base with all levels within the organisation. They take the time to build relationships and forge alliances of interest with others both internally and externally. To the outsider it may seem effortless, but these managers make the effort to actively schedule informal meeting occasions in order to keep a finger on the pulse.

Moving beyond a culture of success or failure

The blame culture has no place in the effective manager's style. They are willing to explore all possibilities that present themselves through external networking and alliances alongside collaboration and empowerment of their team. They seek excellence, learning and development in all aspects of the business and encourage others to do so as a matter of routine.

Decision-making – the buck stops here

One of the necessary abilities that employees identified for their manager to be effective was decisive qualities. The decision-making process can be the loneliest place for a manager to find himself at times. Although it is essential that managers empower others within the organisation to aid the process of decision-making, it is important that the process is concluded in the best possible way. Most important, the responsibility of the decision lies with the manager.

TIP

The buck stops at the effective manager's desk!

There are different ways in differing situations in which everyone goes about making decisions. Research over the past three decades has shown that there are six basic styles used to make decisions:

(1) **Logical**.
(2) **Intuitive**.
(3) **Compliant**.

(4) **No thought**.

(5) **Emotional**.

(6) **Hesitant**.

Questions

◆ How do you currently make decisions?

◆ Are you likely to use one style more than the others?

◆ Do you need to take a more balanced way of decision-making in the workplace?

Logical

Weighing up the evidence and making a decision based on the facts alone is a traditional analytical business process for making decisions: 'There are X, Y and Z options available to us at this time.' It is also a normal decision-making style in an emergency.

Limitations: This can be a very limited way on which to base a decision.

Intuitive

A decision made on gut instinct. It is a well known fact that lasting impressions are made in the first few seconds of meetings between strangers.

Limitations: Whether true or false, those first impressions have a lasting influence which may be proved unfounded.

Compliant

Decisions that are made to 'go with the flow'. The decision has been taken to keep the status quo, to get others happy.

Limitations: If a decision is reached this way in a group, there may be some members present who are basing their decision on the 'no thought' style, or that there is no true debate and empowerment of the individuals by the manager.

No thought

This comes about because whatever the decision, the outcome is of no real interest or benefit to them. 'I know we need a new brochure. Just let me know when you have decided what you want and how much and I will okay whatever you decide. Settle it yourselves.'

Limitations: on the one hand this can be a very empowering approach. On the other hand it can cover up an indecisive manner, adding pressure in the future if the manager decides there is time later to come back and add belated opinions.

Emotional

'The intended pipeline is targeted to go through areas of archaeological interest. We cannot risk any damage, whatever the cost.' Corporate social responsibility is now high on the agenda of companies. To be able to look at decisions from an emotional point of view, rather than a pure business stance, is an important 21st century skill that needs to be developed without the drama and blinkered approach of a purely emotional response.

Limitations: Emotions can cloud business issues.

Hesitant

'We need to cut the budget by X amount, but if we lay employees off think of the lost industry knowledge. Will we be better off with lower costs, but loss of competitive knowledge?'

Limitations: Hesitant decision-making has the power to become procrastination which has the habit of delaying decisions until they are an emergency.

Decision-making techniques

The pros and cons list

For many the process of physically writing down thoughts, questions, and concerns is the beginning of getting all those untidy thoughts that dominate the day out of the mind, and beginning the process of seeing it on paper for reflection.

Questions to ask are

◆ What are the effects of these likely to be?

◆ What are the advantages and disadvantages?

◆ Are there any time lines for when actions and decisions need to be taken?

◆ Who and what else will be affected?

Find a sounding board

Before making decisions, find someone you trust as a sounding board for your thoughts, assumptions and conclusions. Asking for help and support is not a sign of weakness, but a sign of the willingness to recognise no one person can know everything, and that life is one long learning process. This sounding board can be a peer, mentor or executive coach.

Executive coaching
In many cases companies offer the services of an executive coach to their managers to develop their decision-making techniques. It should be a totally confidential relationship between the coach and the coachee, even though the company is paying for the service. It is important to stress here that a coaching relationship is non-dependent, and that it is used to develop the skills of the coachee to perform in the best ways possible for them in the business arena. It is a time specific relationship too. Coaching is for a limited time, on average six months, and not, as in many cases of mentoring, for prolonged periods of time.

TIP

Executive coaching is a supportive relationship to incorporate the knowledge gained into future business process.

PROBLEM-SOLVING – TAKING THE DRAMA OUT OF A CRISIS

The old adage 'don't come with just the problem without bringing solutions' is an intelligent one. For many the word 'problem' in itself produces a feeling of drama and impending crisis that can freeze the mind of coherent thought.

Too many managers are tempted to solve everything themselves. They do not like to give the power to others to develop and think solutions through. A manager who does not trust or who likes to control all around them is not effective. Another old saying, 'two heads are better than one' is certainly never more true than when you have a problem that needs attention. With those who have established a great working relationship, the process of getting together, being honest and respecting each others' views is a normal action. They easily arrive at a point of resolution that each is responsible for, has built-in accountability and can be reviewed if necessary. That is good problem-solving.

A framework to look at problem-solving
What works at the most basic level – even if the problem overshadows the solution? Whether the problem is a recurrent one, new, unforeseen, pressing or irritating there is always a degree of drama that creeps in. Here are some questions to ask yourself that will help to give points of reference embedded in the reality of the situation.

Three steps to successful problem-solving
Step one. Stop and give yourself and others space and time to reflect. Can you discuss it now this minute, or is it something that can be scheduled in for focused thinking time? In the words of Leo from the *West Wing* series based on the US president and the White House, 'It's not an emergency, but it is time-sensitive.'

Step two. Make a quick gauge of the language being used to present the problem.

◆ Is it dramatic: 'It's a complete ****** mess . . .'

◆ Is it emotional: 'Well, Bob's done it again! How come the

stupid so and so always manages to be the one to **** it up?'

◆ Is it personal: 'This is the last straw – I just can't cope with this any more!'

◆ Is it well considered and constructive, bringing with the problem suggestions for possible solutions?

Step three. What scale of problem is this? Is it an emergency or an issue? For example:

◆ Immediate action emergency > The building is on fire and everyone needs to be evacuated now.

◆ Time-sensitive emergency > The wrong information is about to be printed on 100,0000 brochures that are due to be sent out by the end of the week. Someone needs to take responsibility that the correction will be made and act accordingly.

◆ Personality problems > Nothing is more destructive to the effective working of the office than personality clashes, either internally or externally with clients. There may be an immediate problem to be resolved. As the manager you will need to work with this in the short, medium and long term, keeping notes and creating accountability.

◆ Recurrent problem > An important piece of equipment keeps breaking. A permanent solution needs to be found which entails getting all the interested parties together to agree how they can schedule workloads and cover for the period of maintenance, and how they can ensure they will not be negatively affected in future.

◆ Office environment issue > Reassessment to make sure the department is running efficiently and cutting over-heads in the process.

An effective manager will be responsible and ensure that there is a calm, organised environment created within which a resolution can be found. They will have developed those around them to be confident and empowered to create solutions themselves that they can bounce off their manager for a reality check. The effective manager will also allay any conflict and negative emotion that may make a drama into a resolvable problem.

SUMMARY

◆ Know what role you are expected to take within the organisation.

◆ Build relationships and forge alliances internally and externally.

◆ Give 100% to your work and expect 100% from others – and live a balanced life.

◆ Get the broader picture in mind and do not be bogged down in detail and routine office tasks.

◆ Develop a healthy decision-making process and be responsible for the outcome.

◆ Resolve problems without creating a drama.

(3)

Recruiting and Selecting the Right People

Finding and hiring the best applicant for a job is no easy task. With lots of people looking for work, it is challenging to work out how to pick the best person from a large number of candidates. Whether you are about to hire your first employee, or you have taken on staff many times before, you know the feeling. It can be a leap in the dark.

Anyone who wants their business to grow sooner or later needs to take on staff. There comes a time when outsourcing has reached its limits, there is no time to finish the countless tasks – accounts, sales figure analysis, answering the phone, mailing to potential customers – not to mention the VAT return. More hands are needed without doubt – and to make the task seem less daunting (taking into account the growing complexity of the government's employment laws) we need to proceed with care.

Let's look at the various steps involved in the recruitment process.

DEFINING THE JOB TO BE DONE

Analysing the job and drafting the job description

NOTE

The creation of a clear and tangible job description is an essential first step.

Investing time at this stage is a good policy. Whether the position is a new one or you are filling an existing one, before starting the recruiting process be sure you know what standards you are going to use to measure your candidates.

Write down the description of the job, whether it is a newly created post or an existing position. What is the job title? What are the objectives and purpose of the job? What duties, responsibilities and tasks go with it? How does it fit with existing jobs? Where will it lead and what prospects can be offered? What reward package will be offered, salary, benefits etc? Describe the reporting lines and working relationships. State the specific tasks, standards and responsibilities required. Detail the appraisal procedure and be clear as to the remuneration package and other benefits.

While a clear job description is fundamental to successful recruitment, the personal profile sets out the characteristics of the kind of person who might be qualified and suited to undertake the role.

TIP

People are the core of any business. Some people love their jobs and others live for their work.

Consider the salesman who is driven to sell, or the receptionist who enjoys meeting and greeting people.

SPECIFYING THE PROFILE OF THE CANDIDATE

Identifying the characteristics of the person who is most likely to be suitable for the position is useful. Descriptions such as hard working, good attitude, experienced, stable, smart and responsible spring to mind. But how do we find such paragons?

Personal characteristics: This covers age, qualifications, experience, special skills, such as fluency in a foreign language and basic personal characteristics. The purpose here is to make the selection process manageable. Most employers wish to trawl a fairly wide area, but they are not keen to plough through hundreds of applications, most of which are unsuitable.

Character traits: Do you want someone creative, industrious, loyal or innovative? Aspects of character, such as these, are important attributes but much more difficult to measure accurately.

Motivational factors: Will the job suit someone who wants a steady routine or someone who wants something more challenging? The manager needs to look here at what is likely to appeal to an applicant about the job. Is it suitable for someone who is ambitious, competitive, innovative and creative? These are set as a guide only.

Responsibility: Areas of responsibility relate to the aspects of character which make a candidate suitable for the post. Does the applicant have the ability to work on their own, care for others or give presentations to large audiences? Will they need to work as part of a team? Is 100% accuracy essential in their work?

The worst case scenario is to end up appointing someone who proves not able to do the job but not so bad that they can be sacked. It is important to consider the kind of person you feel best suited to the position. Once you have given some time to these details, you can start the selection process.

ATTRACTING THE RIGHT PERSON

There are various ways of accessing potential candidates, one of the most effective sources is:

Internal selection

Via the HR or personnel department, place an internal advertisement of the position. Provided an effective training and selection programme is in place, it is possible to source and select for the new position from within the company. The advantage here is that the applicant is known to the manager. The applicant knows the company and has 'bought-in' to the culture of the firm. It is good for staff morale to see that inside promotion is possible. Only after you have exhausted your internal candidates should you look outside the company.

Referrals

If you are looking to fill a vacancy, make sure you let people know. Whether it is co-workers, colleagues, friends, relatives or clients – many good candidates are sourced from referrals from someone whom you know can give you great insights into the applicant's strengths and weaknesses and character. You will get far more information than you would from CVs alone.

External advertising

When writing a job advertisement, make sure the copy describes the actual job to be done, and describes the organisation in terms of what it does and its style and culture. It also needs to state clearly a specific salary range and the nature and qualifications of the candidates sought. Situations vacant advertisements are relatively inexpensive and can get your job publicised over a wide area. This may have its advantages but the disadvantage is that you may have to sort through literally hundreds of applications to find a few good ones to shortlist.

Temporary agencies

Hiring a temp gives you some relief if the work is piling up while the recruitment process is underway. It also provides the opportunity to try out employees before you hire them. If you like your temp, ask the agency if you can hire them for a nominal fee or after a certain period of time.

Recruitment Consultants

These can be used for sourcing applicants for a specialised position or if you simply do not have the time to go through the whole process of recruitment and selection yourself. The agency carries out the advertising, recruiting and screening of applicants, providing you with a shortlist of perhaps five people to interview.

Executive selection and headhunters

The higher the level of the position you are seeking to fill, the more appropriate it may be to seek assistance from one of the executive search companies of headhunters. They have great experience and are able to select candidates to the highest standard.

The internet

It is possible to use the internet as an effective advertisement. Web pages allow you to present large amounts of information on your company and your job opportunities. The internet is available 24/7 and reaches a huge audience.

Assessing written personal details, including CVs and application forms

When considering applicants' CVs (Curriculum Vitae) bear in mind they can be quite distinctive:

◆ A targeted CV draws attention to the applicant's skills and focuses on the qualities that make them the right person for the particular position.

◆ A chronological CV is one that summarises the qualifications and career experience of the candidate. This form of CV is popular with local authorities, central government and more traditional employers.

◆ An experience-based CV is valid for individuals who work in specialised areas of employment. It describes their track record to date.

◆ CVs should be precise and list a candidate's achievements with detailed points. Beware CVs which generalise – this could indicate a weak candidate.

◆ There is no need for large amounts of personal detail to be added to a CV. It should be a piece of personal marketing literature – focusing on the product – in other words the skill the candidate offers.

◆ CVs which are gimmicky are risky. A CV should look attractive, clean and professional. Trendy typefaces and coloured ink are not appropriate. If a CV contains spelling mistakes, it could indicate a careless individual.

◆ Be vigilant at checking accuracy of CVs – employment history, qualifications and skills.

A SYSTEMATIC APPROACH TO INTERVIEWING

TIP

When it comes to interviewing candidates, you do need to ask the right questions.

Because hiring the right people is essential to the growth and success of your business, the manager needs to get the interview techniques right. This means asking loaded questions which will reveal the information you need to make an informed decision.

At the outset welcome the applicant, then begin by summarising the position. Ask the prepared questions and use the candidate's answers to evaluate strengths and weaknesses. Conclude the interview after allowing the candidate the opportunity to ask any questions he or she wishes. Advise them when you will be making your selection.

Take time to prepare your questions and make notes of the applicant's answers:

'Why are you here?'
This may elicit the answer 'because I want a job with your firm'. But it could give you other information, which you would never have gleaned had you not asked in the first place.

'What can you do for us?'
An important question and one for which candidates should be prepared. It is quite common for applicants today to

approach the recruitment process on the basis of 'what can your company do for me?' and this question redresses the balance.

'What kind of person are you?'
You need to know – after all, if recruited you will be spending considerable periods of time in their company. You want to employ someone who will be congenial most of the time they are at work.

'If you stayed with your current company, what would be your next move?'
This is a question designed to extract information on several levels. It should reveal a sense of what the applicant expects but also why the applicant wants to move on. If, for example, the applicant says they want to be a manager but the person above has been there for 25 years, you can move on with the interview. If they were to say that they hoped to be promoted within six months, why are they leaving that job? You should try to elicit the real reason for wanting to leave that company.

'What do you consider makes you exceptional compared to others?'
A difficult question for most people, because applicants have a tendency to be uncomfortable praising themselves. If the answer is given in a reasoned manner, the applicant may have a good degree of self-esteem and some courage. A timid response could indicate a reticent type – not one fit for a challenging role within your company. Beware the applicant who launches into a lengthy monologue about why the world revolves around them. The over-active ego could

spell disaster if the applicant is aiming to fill a position where teamwork is a requisite.

'Describe your greatest achievement to date.'
If the applicant can recall quickly and with detail a satisfying and recently accomplished project, which they recount in a measured, comprehensive way, you may have a winner here. Any applicant who is quick enough to think on their feet and produce the anecdote without hesitation is likely to be an asset to your company.

'Do you need many hours a week to get your work done?'
This question is designed to elicit the work ethic of the potential employee. If they expect to put in long hours with your company, this could indicate staying late to do extra work, or merely that they work inefficiently. A discussion as to working habits can reveal how they will fit in with the rest of the employees. A company where it is normal to stay until 7pm would not suit someone with a strict 9 to 5 mind set.

'What sort of salary are you expecting?'
There is no point in having gone through the selection process only to reach the end of the interview and find out that your idea of a competitive salary and benefits package is so far removed from the candidate's that you seem to be on different planets. You may not be able to offer enough in terms of salary, but try putting together a generous benefits package – including pleasant office, corporate membership of a health club, impressive job title, generous holidays, health insurance, pension etc.

> **TIP**
>
> Keep notes as you interview each of the candidates. It will be impossible to remember who said what and your written notes will be an essential aid when evaluating the applicants.

There are one or two topics on which it is not appropriate to question applicants: these relate to the applicant's race, skin colour or national origin, anything to do with marital status, religion and criminal record. Personal details such as height, weight, financial status and disabilities are also not necessary. These questions do not relate to how the applicants perform their jobs and are best avoided.

Assessment and checks

Check, check and check again. References, skills, previous employment history. Do the dates on the CV match with other facts? Was that extended holiday actually spent at Her Majesty's pleasure?

It is quite surprising how many people exaggerate their education experience. This is a good place to start your checks. If it is found that the application is inaccurate about one thing, it is likely that the rest of their CV is too.

Don't be hesitant about calling previous employers for information about an applicant. You should get more detail from a supervisor or manager than from the HR or personnel department, who is more likely simply to confirm the dates the applicant was employed.

With regard to skills, if the job requires good presentation skills you could ask the applicant to give a short talk. If they need to write well, look at some examples of their written work. If the requirement is for fluent French, set an oral test.

FINAL SELECTION AND APPOINTMENT

When reviewing the information about all the candidates, you will be glad to look at the notes you made. (You did take notes, surely?) How does each applicant stand up against your original criteria for the position? Is there an outright winner? How many losers? Sort them into categories: Winners, possible winners and losers. Be objective. Don't be influenced by irrelevant elements such as clothes or hairstyles.

◆ If there is more than one candidate with equally good qualifications, it may be necessary to go for a second or third round of interviews. This may seem time-consuming or expensive, but it is better than making a wrong appointment and living to regret it.

◆ If you really can't be sure – go with your gut instincts. Although they may seem equally matched in skills and experience, you will probably have a feeling that one is more suitable than the other. If so, allow your intuition free reign.

◆ It is sometimes wise to hire people for their personalities rather than for their skills and qualifications. Whereas it is difficult to change someone's personality, it is not impossible to teach them new skills or train them in certain techniques.

◆ If in doubt, don't be afraid to ask for advice. Managers hiring staff must be certain of the decision they are about to make. Ask your mentor, or an experienced director of a well-established company. Managers of small businesses or new ventures cannot afford to make mistakes and most people are happy to help if requested to do so.

◆ Never hire someone on the basis that 'he's the best of a bad bunch'. This is potentially disastrous. Better to repeat the whole process again because rarely do people make a miraculous change for the better once they are appointed.

Once you have made your decision, telephone the successful applicant as soon as possible and offer your first choice the job and secure their acceptance. If they are no longer available go to candidate B. Hopefully you will be able to hire someone from amongst your selection of 'winners'.

Don't forget to communicate with the unsuccessful candidates. It maybe old-fashioned courtesy, but it costs nothing to be polite. It will make them feel a lot better. A short letter to them saying you will consider alternatives (if they might suit another position in the company) or that you are keeping their CV on file (and telling them you are doing so).

TIP

Don't forget that if your business grows the way it should, your new employee could be a manager one day.

They will be running the office in your absence. By looking for someone who possesses that extra spark, someone who would be happy to take responsibility and act on their own initiative, you could be choosing your successor!

Some helpful hints on interpreting employee qualities

Outgoing personality	*Always away from the office*
Good communication skills	*Spends a lot of time on the phone*
Average employee	*Not too bright*
Exceptionally well qualified	*Made no major blunders yet*
Work is first priority	*Too ugly to get a date*
Active socially	*Drinks a lot*
Family is active socially	*Spouse drinks too*
Independent worker	*Nobody knows what he/she does*
Quick thinker	*Offers plausible excuses*
Careful thinker	*Won't make a decision*
Aggressive	*Obnoxious*
Uses logic on difficult jobs	*Gets someone else to do it*
Expresses themselves well	*Speaks English*
Meticulous attention to detail	*A nit picker*
Has leadership qualities	*Is tall and has a loud voice*

4

Managing People

Managing people is something that we often think we can do, or indeed ought to be able to do. The interesting thing is that it is neither something we have been trained to do, nor something we have necessarily learnt or been taught to do. People are generally employed for their skills, not their management capabilities. For instance, a salesman or saleswoman is employed for his or her selling skills. As time goes by they will improve those skills and perhaps become the number one salesman/woman in the company.

Overnight they are promoted to sales manager or even sales director. Their selling skills are suddenly redundant. What they need now is management skills. But what if they haven't got those skills? This could be a very traumatic experience that threatens all their existing patterns of behaviour and lifestyle. Some people are fortunate enough to be offered management training but the vast majority are not. They have no choice but to muddle through, copy other people or emulate a role model, all of whom may have had to do precisely that in their own past.

This chapter tackles two of the foundation stones of effective management practice:

◆ **delegation** and

◆ **appraisals**

both of which are critical to developing and improving performance in others.

DELEGATION

Delegate (v. tr.) 1 to entrust (eg a duty or responsibility) to another. 2 to appoint (somebody) as one's representative. (v. intr.) to assign responsibility or authority to other people.

Delegation is a word that is bandied about liberally and something that people pay lip service to. People rarely delegate effectively. Mostly what happens is that people get *told* to do a job or take something on – that is not delegation. Very often it is an either/or situation. Either they get dumped with something they can't cope with or they don't get a chance to prove their worth because delegation is not implemented effectively. More often than not it hasn't been thought through, which results in things going wrong, breakdowns, upsets and so on. All very de-motivating for staff and managers alike.

As managers you will have to assign or allocate work to others in your team(s). This will be done by balancing the work that has to be done against the availability of people and their abilities. Some of the work may be routine and repetitive; some may not.

When you assign work to a team member, you may retain the decision-making responsibility if it becomes necessary to decide upon an alternative course of action. Delegation goes one step further and implies that the authority to make decisions is given to the team member.

NOTE

Delegation develops others.

If you cannot delegate effectively you will find your own development will suffer and you will become snowed under with work. You need to recognise the importance of delegating work to others in your team so that they too can develop and grow.

Some reasons for not delegating

There are several reasons why managers feel reluctant to delegate. The most frequent excuse I come across is: 'It's easier to do it myself.' That may be true to start with but it soon becomes a vicious circle: the more you have to do, the easier it is to do it all yourself because it is quicker than taking the time to delegate. But that road leads to overload for you and loss of morale for others. Ask yourself what might be preventing you from delegating; is it that you:

◆ do not understand the need to delegate

◆ lack confidence in team members and therefore will not give them the authority for decision-making

◆ do not know how to delegate effectively

◆ have tried to delegate in the past, but failed and so will not try again

◆ like doing a particular job which should be delegated, but will not delegate it even though you know the team member would enjoy the job

◆ do not understand the management role or how to go about it

◆ are frightened of making yourself dispensable, so keep hold of every job

◆ think you have no time to delegate

◆ have nobody to delegate to.

All of these barriers need to be overcome if you are to delegate effectively.

Exercise

What may stop you from delegating?

List four reasons why you find it difficult to delegate.

The skill of delegating

Delegation is a skill like any other skill and one that can very quickly be learned. Most of it is common sense, but here are some tips for effective delegation:

◆ Plan delegation well in advance.

◆ Think through exactly what you want done. Define a precise aim.

◆ Consider the degree of guidance and support needed by the delegates.

TIP

Delegation and trust go hand in hand.

◆ Pitch the briefing appropriately. Check understanding.

◆ Establish review dates. Check understanding.

◆ Establish a 'buffer' period at the end, in which failings can be put right.

◆ Delegate whole jobs wherever possible, rather than bits and pieces.

◆ Inform others who are involved.

◆ Having delegated, stand back. Do not 'hover'.

◆ Recognise work may not be done exactly as you would have done it. Do not nit-pick.

◆ Delegate, not abdicate, responsibility.

What should be delegated

A manager must analyse the job he/she is actually doing in order to establish what can and cannot be delegated. One way of doing this is by using a time diary (see Chapter 1). This will show you:

◆ Totally unnecessary tasks which need not be done at all.

◆ Work which should be done by another person or in another department.

◆ Time-consuming tasks not entailing much decision-making which, providing training is given, could be done as well by the team member as by the manager.

◆ Repetitive tasks which over a period take up a considerable amount of time, but require more decision-making and would serve to help develop a team member.

A delegation plan and timetable must then be proposed to enable time to be found to delegate. Except for the simplest of jobs, you will find that something like eight to twelve times longer will be needed to delegate a job effectively than to actually do it. Here's the rub! However, by taking the time to delegate properly in the first place you will save yourself far more time in the future. See it as an investment in your own future as well as in the future development of the delegate.

'The individual is the key to personal and organisational success.'

What should not be delegated

There are always certain tasks and authorities which a manager must not delegate. This does not mean that he or she cannot employ staff to assist with these areas of work, but he/she does remain the final decision-maker. These areas of work are:

- Being forward looking and constantly seeking opportunities for the enterprise.

- Setting aims and objectives.

- Creating high achievement plans for his/her enterprise or the part of it for which he/she is responsible and ensuring quality standards are developed and maintained.

- Coordinating activity – that is knowing the task that has to be done, the abilities and needs of his/her people, the resources available and then blending them to achieve optimum results.

- Communicating with his/her people and with senior managers and colleagues.

- Providing leadership and positive motivation.

- The training and development of his/her team.

- Monitoring and surveying everything that is going on and taking action necessary to maintain the planned level of achievement and quality performance.

From the above, it is clear that no manager will weaken his/her position by delegating work which does not fall into any of these areas.

The contrary will also be true. The managers will free themselves to do the jobs that they alone can and should do, to be effective.

NOTE

Remember: delegate not abdicate.

HOW TO DELEGATE

Once a delegation plan has been prepared, each job must be taken separately. The manager must then prepare a specification which will state:

◆ The objective or intended goal of the job.

◆ The method the manager has developed to do it.

◆ Data requirements and where the information comes from.

◆ Any aids or equipment needed to do the work.

◆ Define boundaries of responsibilities.

◆ The principal categories of decisions that have to be made.

◆ Any limitations on authority given to make these decisions. Namely, when the manager should be consulted.

When this preliminary specification has been prepared, the manager must start coaching or training the delegate to do the job. Initially, close control should be maintained, but this should be loosened as soon as possible. Some form of control must be maintained, but this should not be more than is necessary to ensure that the job continues to be done properly. Keep track of which jobs you have delegated and to whom. Monitor the process with each delegate from a tactful distance.

Advantages to team members

Delegation is often seen as being of advantage to the manager but it is also of considerable benefit to the team member. The fact that jobs which have been developed by a manager are passed to others to do, and the requisite authority to act is also given to them, is an aid to the development of individuals both practically and psychologically.

A good delegator or a willing martyr?

Delegation is one of the most difficult things a busy director must learn. Take the test below to see what kind of delegator you are.

1. *What does delegation mean to you?*
(a) Passing the buck to juniors
(b) Dumping responsibilities
(c) Tricking others into doing work that is rightfully yours
(d) None of the above

2. *Why are you nervous about delegating?*
(a) You do not trust anyone else to do the work
(b) You do not want to overburden someone else
(c) You have not got time to train or prepare others
(d) Overwork is part of your job

3. *What word would you most associate with delegation?*
(a) Risk
(b) Fear
(c) Guilt
(d) Trust

4. *If you did delegate a task or tasks, which would they be?*
(a) The most boring ones
(b) The least risky ones
(c) The most risky ones
(d) The ones that a subordinate could do just as well

5. *If you had to delegate an important job to a subordinate, how would you do it?*

(a) Issue it as an order

(b) Be very apologetic

(c) Leave it to someone else to convey

(d) Present it as an opportunity

6. *When delegating to someone, which of these apply to you?*

(a) Keep worrying that the job is not being done well

(b) Ask them to report back each time a decision is made

(c) Stipulate that if anything goes wrong, it is their responsibility

(d) Tell them only to come back to you if there is a problem they cannot handle.

Effective delegation is about trusting your staff and colleagues and delegating authority – but not responsibility. If you answered 'd' to each question, you need read no further.

Question 1: Delegation should never be forced on others, nor presented in a negative way. At best it is an opportunity for career development. However much you delegate, the buck always stops with you.

Question 2: If you do not trust your staff, you cannot truly delegate – you will always be involved in their judgements. It is all about learning to respect and trust your team so that tasks can be more evenly spread.

Question 3: Delegation = Trust.

Delegation exercise

As you read through the list below, tick any items that you feel particularly apply to you.

Then consider whether the suggested changes in what you do might be helpful.

Barriers to delegating	How you might tackle the barrier
◆ I find it difficult to ask people to do things.	Try explaining to them what you will be freed to do if they take on the task.
◆ I do not have time to delegate.	Decide to break out of the vicious circle and make time. By investing, say, half an hour explaining the task you save, say, the three hours it will take to do the task.
◆ It is quicker to do the job myself; explaining it to someone else takes too much time.	It may be quicker to do the job yourself, but you have a responsibility to develop your staff members' skills. They will get quicker with practice.
◆ I could do the job better.	Being responsible for developing the skills of your staff means investing time in development and training. In the long run it will save time. Set up a development programme.

◆ I need to know exactly what is happening.

As a manager, you must get results through other people, or you will become overloaded – so you need to trust your staff. Build in regular feedback.

◆ I enjoy this job. I've always done it.

As a manager, you have to let go of tasks that other staff can do. Do only what you can and should do.

◆ I am afraid it won't get done properly, and I will get the blame.

Prepare for delegation, and build in controls as the job is done. You have the right to make mistakes.

◆ I am afraid someone else will do it better than I can.

Set targets for your team members to do better than you at specific tasks.

◆ They will not do it my way.

Agree to goals and targets and give freedom. There are often many ways of doing a job. A good team benefits from a variety of approaches.

◆ I am not sure how to do this task so feel I had better do it myself.

You need to decide how to tackle the task before deciding whether it's suitable to delegate.

◆ The job is too big/important.

Break the job down. All jobs contain some routine elements which can be delegated.

Question 4: Delegating the worst jobs is not worthy of the name. You should delegate tasks that you would normally be able and prepared to do. It is not an excuse for offloading rotten jobs.

Question 5: Good delegation needs to be presented as a positive benefit. How you 'sell' delegated tasks is most important. You should delegate the interesting and challenging jobs – and negotiate with the delegate.

Question 6: Learn to let go. If you trust your subordinates, let them run with a task. If you feel any doubts about their capabilities, invest in training and staff development – it's cheaper than you suffering from stress-related illness.

PERFORMANCE APPRAISALS

Appraisal (n) an act or instance of appraising e.g. a valuation of property by an authorised person, or an assessment of a worker's performance.

Appraisals are all too often the bane of a working life rather than something to look forward to and enjoy. Appraisals should be a win/win experience: both parties should gain by it and feel a sense of satisfaction and achievement. They are an opportunity for both managers and staff to assess each others' performance, build relationship and receive constructive feedback. Appraisals should be conducted once a year as an absolute minimum, with less formal quarterly reviews or appraisals in the interim.

The benefits to the individual

◆ discussion of the job role in the context of a job description

◆ assessing performance against agreed objectives

◆ opportunity to give and receive feedback

◆ having training needs identified

◆ opportunity to discuss career prospects and promotion

◆ future planning – understanding and agreeing objectives

◆ building relationship

◆ reinforcing the delegation process

◆ on-the-spot coaching

◆ increase motivation and improve morale.

Benefits to the line manager

◆ evaluating performance (individual, team, organisation)

◆ making the best use of resources

◆ giving constructive feedback

◆ setting and clarifying objectives

◆ identification of training needs

◆ audit of team's strengths and weaknesses

◆ receiving feedback on management style

◆ exploring and resolving problems

◆ reducing staff turnover.

Benefits to the company

◆ improved performance through commitment to employees

◆ a minimum standard of good management

◆ collation of training needs

◆ manpower and succession planning

◆ test of selection process

◆ reduction in staff turnover

◆ improvement in morale and motivation.

Preparation for the discussion

Preparation for the interview is essential if both parties are going to get the most out of it. You will need to think carefully about what you want to discuss, gather relevant information and focus on relevant issues. You will need to notify the person in writing and familiarise yourself with the individual's file and performance factors.

You will also need to think about the environment in which you conduct the appraisal. A neutral location is generally better than your office or theirs. Make sure that you have what you need in the room – water, tea, coffee – ensure that you are both (all) comfortable and that you will not be interrupted. And be sure to allow enough time.

NOTE

Appraisals are a two way process.

CONDUCTING THE INTERVIEW

During the interview:

◆ start on a positive note – emphasise what is working

◆ use the ten to one ratio for feedback – ten positives to one negative

◆ create a relaxed, positive atmosphere

◆ review the purpose of the interview

◆ use an agenda

◆ encourage the manager/role holder to talk

◆ listen carefully

◆ use open questions

◆ keep to the agenda during the interview

◆ ensure you cover all the key aspects of the role

◆ discuss areas for improvement

◆ avoid over-criticising

◆ deal with one topic at a time

◆ summarise and maintain control throughout

◆ discuss further training and career development needs

◆ review and summarise main points, agree action plans

◆ end on a positive note, thank each other for your contributions.

Good question!

Open question Comparative Hypothetical Focused Reflective Link	Use to develop discussion and explore issues and alternatives
Closed question	Use to uncover facts or confirm feelings
Leading question Multiple Forced choice	Do not use

For further examples and information on asking questions
see p. 142–145, Directing a Communication.

Active listening

Active	*Passive*
L Look interested	Show no encouraging responses
I Involve yourself by questioning	Ask irrelevant questions or assume

S Stay on target	Become distracted or daydream
T Test your understanding	Do not clarify or summarise
E Evaluate the message	Do not connect/relate to other information
N Neutralise your feelings	Have prejudices and make snap judgements

Constructive feedback

When giving constructive feedback remember to:

◆ balance praise and criticism – ten to one ratio

◆ be constructive

◆ be factual and specific

◆ maintain open communication

◆ focus on behaviour not personality

◆ be prepared to give and receive

◆ be honest

◆ agree future changes/solutions.

After the interview, complete all documentation and confirm all agreements made during the meeting. Send these to the appraisee and copies to your HR department as well as your own file.

NOTE

Appraisals can be fun!

Appraisals can be opportunities for change on the one hand, or they can be a damaging experience on the other. They can make the difference between a high performing and motivated work force and one that does the bare minimum to get by. I know which one I would choose!

IN SUMMARY

Delegation
Key action points:

◆ Invest time in **people**.

◆ **Anticipate**: strategy – competition problems

◆ **Think** about: tomorrow – outstanding work – delegation.

◆ **Plan** 'A' time work four weeks ahead.

◆ Establish **start** times.

◆ **Delegate**: good for you and your team.

◆ **Meetings**: small agenda – small attendance – precise actions – punctual finish.

TIP

Meetings: NO AOB!

◆ Keep your secretary/clerical support **in the picture**.

◆ Filing system: easy **retrieval**.

◆ Keep your desk for **work not storage**.

Appraisee's charter
I have the right to:

◆ receive my appraisal when it is due

◆ be clear what is expected from me

◆ have feedback on my performance

◆ gather my own evidence

◆ make genuine mistakes

◆ contribute equally to agreeing objectives and standards

◆ raise issues and concerns

◆ consult others.

Appraiser's charter
I have the right to:

◆ give feedback on performance

◆ contribute equally to objectives and standards

◆ consult others

◆ say 'no' to unreasonable requests

◆ adjourn the performance discussion

◆ expect certain standards of work and behaviour.

5

Getting the Most from People

Motivate (v.tr) 1 supply a motive to: be the motive of. 2 cause (a person) to act in a particular way. 3 stimulate the interest of (a person in an activity).

If you think you can, you can and if you think you can't, you're right. This was said by Mary Kay Ash. It is fair comment. Motivation matters. There is considerable research to show that people who are, to put it simply, happy in their work will perform better than those who are not. As the job of the manager is about getting results *through* other people, rather than for them, the motivational state is important. In terms of both productivity and quality of action maximising motivational feeling will assist performance. Similarly, it is easy for any dilution of motivation to act to reduce performance; something that ultimately reflects on the manager. Multiply the effects, either positive or negative, by the number of people reporting to you and you see the real importance.

Managers must act not just to ensure that people perform well, but to ensure they do so consistently and reliably.

Good motivation also acts to make sure that people are as self-sufficient as possible, able to make decisions – good decisions – on their own and take action to keep things running smoothly. If you have to check every tiny detail and issue moment by moment instructions, then neither productivity nor the quality achieved are likely to be as good as they might be. There is every difference in the world between people being able to do something and do it well, however, and being willing to do it and do it well.

Thus managers need to motivate people, rather than leave them to their own devices. Motivation, like so much else in management, does not just happen. It must be recognised as an active process – one that you need to allow some time for on a continuing basis.

THE FUNDAMENTALS OF MOTIVATION
The theory of motivation is extensive and this is not the place to do other than recap some essential principles (if you are entirely familiar with the principles, then by all means skip to the next main heading).

The essentials of motivating successfully
Many people, certainly in years gone by, took the view that getting performance from staff was a straightforward pro-cess. You told them what to do, and they did it. Period. And

if that was, for some reason, insufficient then it was backed by the power of management; effectively by coercion.

Management by fear still exists. In any economy with less than full employment the ultimate threat is being out of a job. But whether the threat is subtle or specific, whether it is just an exaggerated form of arm-twisting or out and out bullying, even if it works (at least short-term) – it is resented. Your job as a manager is not simply to get things done, it is to get things done willingly.

The resentment factor is considerable. People fight against anything they consider to be an unreasonable demand. So much so that the fighting may tie up a fair amount of time and effort, with performance ending up as only the minimum people 'think they can get away with'.

> NOTE
>
> Only if people *want* to do things, and are encouraged to do things well, can they be relied on to actually do them really well.

Motivation provides reasons for people to want to deliver good performance. If this sounds no more than common sense, then that is because it is. For example, are you more likely to read on if I tell you that if you do not I will come round to your house and break all your windows, or if I persuade you that you will find doing so really useful and offer you some sort of tangible reward? (I do intend that you will find it useful, incidentally, but sadly there is no free holiday on offer.) Motivation works because it reflects something about human nature, and understanding the various theories about this is a useful prerequisite to deploying motivational techniques and influencing staff behaviour.

Theory X and Theory Y

The first of the classic motivational theories that is worthy of some note was documented by Douglas McGregor. He defined the human behaviour relevant to organisational life as follows:

◆ *Theory X:* makes the assumption that people are lazy, uninterested in work or responsibility and thus must be pushed and cajoled to get anything done in a disciplined way, with reward assisting the process to some degree.

◆ *Theory Y:* takes the opposite view. It assumes people want to work. They enjoy achievement, gain satisfaction from responsibility and are naturally inclined to seek ways of making work a positive experience.

There is truth in both pictures. What McGregor was doing was describing extreme positions. Of course, there are jobs that are inherently boring and mundane, and others that are obviously more interesting and it is no surprise that it is easier to motivate those doing the latter. Though having said that, it is really a matter of perspective. There is an old, and apocryphal, story of a despondent group of convicts breaking rocks being asked about their feelings concerning the back-breaking work. All expressed negative feelings, except one – who said simply 'it makes it bearable if I keep the end result in mind – I'm helping to build a cathedral.'

Whether you favour theory X or Y, and theory Y is surely more attractive, it is suggested that motivation creates a process that draws the best from any situation. Some motivation can help move people from a theory X situation to a theory Y one, thereafter it is easier to build on positive theory Y principles to achieve still better motivational feeling and still better performance; and your communication should reflect this fact.

Maslow's hierarchy of needs

Another theory that helps describe the basic situation on which all motivational effort must be directed is that of Abraham Maslow. He wrote that people's needs were satisfied progressively. In other words, only when basic needs are met do their aspirations rise and other goals are set.

◆ The first such needs were basic: enough to eat and drink, warmth, shelter and rest. In a working environment people need to earn sufficient money to buy the answers to these factors.

◆ Next come needs of safety and protection: ranging from job security (one that is less easily met than once was the case) to good health (with the provision of health care schemes by employers now very common).

◆ Beyond that he described social needs: all those associated with working in groups and with people. The work environment is a social environment, indeed for some people contacts formed through work may represent the majority of the people contacted in their lives.

◆ Linked to these are a further level of needs – psychological ones, such as recognition within the organisation and amongst the people comprising the work environment, and the ability to feel self-confidence, self-fulfilment and look positively to a better future, one in which we are closer to realising our perceived potential and happier because of it.

However you define and describe this theory, it is the hierarchical nature of it that is most important. What it says, again wholly sensibly, is that people's motivations can only be satisfied if this hierarchy is respected. For instance, it suggests that motivational input is doomed to be ineffective if it is directed at one level when a lower one is unsatisfied. It is thus little use to tell people how satisfying a job is, if they are consumed with the thought that the low rate of pay makes them unable to afford basic essentials. Thus all communication with staff designed to have a motivational impact must bear in mind the whole picture.

Again this does not describe the whole process in a way that you can use to create the right motivation in your office, but it helps show one element of what is involved.

Hertzberg's motivator/hygiene factors

This last theory leads to a view of the process that links much more directly to an action based approach to creating positive motivation. Hertzberg described two categories of factor:

◆ first the hygiene factors, those dissatisfiers that switch people off if they cause difficulty

◆ secondly the motivators, factors that can make people feel good.

Consider these in turn:

The dissatisfiers (or hygiene factors)
Hertzberg listed these, in order of their impact, as follows:

◆ company policy and administrative processes

◆ supervision

◆ working conditions

◆ salary

◆ relationship with peers

◆ personal life (and the impact of work on it)

◆ status

◆ security.

All are external factors that affect the individual (because of this they are sometimes referred to as *environmental* factors). When things are without problem in these areas, all is well motivationally. If there are problems they all contain considerable potential for diluting any positive motivational feeling.

It should be noted here, in case it surprises you, that salary comes in this list. It is a potential dissatisfier. Would you fail to raise your hand in answer to the question: would you like to earn more money? Most people would certainly say yes.

At a particular moment an existing salary may be acceptable (or unacceptable), but it is unlikely to turn you on and be a noticeable part of your motivation. So too for those who work for you – more of this later.

It is, for instance, things in these areas that give rise to gripes and to a feeling of dissatisfaction that rumbles on. If the firm's parking scheme fails to work and you always find someone else in your place, perhaps someone more senior who it is difficult to dislodge, it rankles and the feeling is always with you.

There are, as we will see later, many things springing from these areas for managers to work at, and which getting right can see making a positive contribution to boosting the motivational climate.

The restriction here is that these things are not those that can add powerfully to positive motivational feeling. Get things right here and demotivation is avoided. To add more you have to turn to Hertzberg's second list.

The satisfiers (or motivators)
These define the key factors that create positive motivation. They are, in order of relative power:

◆ achievement

◆ recognition

◆ the work itself

◆ responsibility

♦ advancement

♠ growth

It is all these factors, whether positive or negative and stemming from the intrinsic qualities of human nature, that offer the best chance of being used by management to play their part in ensuring that people want to perform and perform well. Communication is a vital part of this picture. Every piece of communication can have motivational over-tones – and probably will. For example, put in a new system, say asking people to fill in a new form on a regular basis, and – if it is not made clear why it is useful – people will be demotivated (because it relates to the list of dissatisfiers – specifically policy and administration – above).

Similarly, a wealth of different communications all affect the motivational climate, jogging the overall measure of it one way or the other, for example:

♦ *Job descriptions, clear guidelines and adequate training:* all give a feeling of security, without which motivation suffers.

♦ *Incentives:* will work less effectively if their details are not clearly communicated (for instance, an incentive pay-ment scheme may be allowed to seem so complicated that no one works out how they are doing and motivation suffers as a result).

♦ *Routine jobs:* can be made more palatable by com-municating to people what an important contribution they make.

◆ *Job titles:* may sensibly be chosen with an eye on how they affect people's feelings of status as well as acting as a description of function ('sales executive' may be fine and clear to customers, but most prefer titles like 'account service manager').

Furthermore, the same essential act can be changed radically in terms of the effect it has motivationally just by varying the way in which communication occurs.

NOTE

The simplest and least expensive positive motivational act a manager can engage in is probably uttering the simple phrase 'Well done'.

Which of us can put a hand on our heart and say we do even that sufficiently often? . . .

Consider some different ways of doing it, listed in what is probably an ascending order of motivational power:

◆ Saying well done, one-to-one.

◆ Saying it in public, in an open plan office, say.

◆ Saying it at an 'occasion' (anything from a departmental meeting to a group taking a coffee break together).

◆ Saying it (in one of the ways listed) and then confirming it in writing.

◆ Getting the initial statement (however it may be done) endorsed by someone senior.

◆ Publishing it (say in a company newsletter).

The implications here are clear. Not only is motivation itself primarily executed through communication, but the precise form of that communication needs to be borne in mind and contributes directly to the effect achieved.

TIP

Sometimes the opportunity to motivate and do so successfully is dependent on the way things are communicated.

The following example reinforces this point.

Turning a big problem into a small one

A travel agent is essentially a service and people business. In one particular firm, with a chain of some 30 retail outlets across several countries, business was lagging behind targets. The industry was, at the time, not in recession, rather the lag was due to competitive activity and was potentially something that a more active, sales oriented approach could potentially cure. Initially the approach to the problem was to draw attention to the problem at every level. Memos were circulated to all staff. The sales revenue planned for the business, the amount coming from holidays, flights etc were substantial figures; even the shortfall was some hundreds of thousands of pounds.

The result? Certainly the sales graph did not rise, but, equally, morale dropped. People went from feeling they worked for a successful organisation to thinking it was – at worst – foundering; and feeling that the fault was being laid at their door. The figures meant little to the kind of young people who manned the counters – they were just unimaginably large numbers to which they were wholly unable to relate personally.

With a sales conference coming, a different strategy was planned. The large shortfall was amortised and presented as a series of smaller figures – one per branch. These 'catch-up' figures were linked to what needed to be sold, in addition to normal business, in order to catch up and hit target. It amounted, if I remember rightly, to two additional holidays (Mum, Dad and 2.2 children) per branch, per week. Not only was this something staff could easily relate to, it was something they understood and felt was possible. Individual targets, ongoing communication to report progress and some prizes for branches hitting and besting these targets in a number of ways completed the picture.

The result this time? The numbers slowly climbed. The gap closed. Motivation increased with success in sight. And a difficult year ended with the company hitting the original planned targets – and motivation continued to run high as a real feeling of achievement was felt.

The key here was, I am sure, one of communication. The numbers and the difficulty of hitting them did not change. The perception of the problem, however, was made manageable, personal and – above all – was made to seem achievable. The results then showed that success was possible. No significant costs were involved here, just a little thought and time to make sure the communications were right, that motivation was positively affected and that results stood a real chance of rising.

In many such circumstances, a positive impact on many problems is made more likely if motivation is used to influence people. As a last thought about this example, it should be said that while the difficulties that were surmounted by the travel company make it a good example, the same principles apply to *positive* situations. It is as important, and often easier, to build on success as to tackle difficulties, indeed this may produce the greatest return for the action taken. But this is only the case if the communication with people is clear, and messages are put in a way that makes them easy to relate to.

PRODUCING POSITIVE RESULTS

It may seem from what has been said already that motivation is a complex business. To some extent this is so. Certainly it is a process affected by many, and disparate, factors. The list of factors affecting motivation, for good or ill, may be long, and that is where any complexity lies, but the process of linking to them in terms of action is often straightforward.

The very nature of people, and how their motivation can be influenced, suggests five important principles for the manager dedicated to actively motivating people. These are:

1. There is no magic formula. No one thing, least of all money, provides an easy option for creating positive motivation at a stroke, and anything that suggests itself as such a panacea should be viewed with suspicion.

2. Success is in the details. Good motivation comes from minimising the factors that tend to create dissatisfaction, and maximising the effect of those factors that can create positive motivation. *All of them* in both cases must be considered; it is a process of leaving no stone unturned, with all those found able to contribute to the overall picture being useful to utilise. At the end of the day, what is described as the motivational climate of an organisation, department or office is the sum of all the pluses and minuses in terms of how individual factors weigh in the balance and communication plays a key role.

3. Continuity. The analogy of climate is a good one. As a small-scale example of this, bear in mind a glasshouse. Many factors contribute to the temperature inside; the heating, windows, window blinds, whether a door or window is open, if heating is switched on and so on. But some such things – whatever they are – are in place and contributing to the prevailing temperature *all the time.* So too with motivation. Managers must accept that creating and maintaining a good motivational climate takes some time and is a continuous task. Anything, perhaps everything, they do can have motivational side effects. For example, as was mentioned, a change of policy may involve a new system and its use may have desirable effects (saving money, say), but if complying with the system is seen as bureaucratic and time consuming the motivational effect may be negative despite results being changed for the better.

Overall the trick is to spend the minimum amount of time in such a way that it secures the maximum positive effect.

4. Time scale. Another thing that must be recognised is the differing time scales involved here. On the one hand signs of low motivation can be a good early warning of performance in peril. If you keep your ear to the ground you may be able to prevent negative shifts in performance or productivity by letting signs of demotivation alert you to the coming problem. The level of motivation falls first, performance follows.

Similarly, watch the signs after you have taken action aimed at actively affecting motivation positively. Performance may take a moment to start to change for the better, but you may well be able to identify that this is likely through the signs of motivation improving. Overreacting because things do not change instantly may do more harm than good. If motivation is improving, performance improvement is usually not far behind.

So the timing of communication is vital too. A busy moment and something allowed to go by default may lead to problems at some point in the future.

5. Bear others in mind. There is a major danger in taking a censorious view of any motivational factor – positive or negative. Most managers find that some at least of the things that worry their staff, or switch them on, are not things that would affect themselves. No matter. It is the other people who matter. If you regularly find things that you are inclined to dismiss as not of any significance, be careful. What matters to you is *not* the same as what matters to others.

If you discover something that can act for you influencing your people, however weird or trivial it may seem, use it. Dismissing it out of hand – and in communication terms, say, failing to explain something adequately – just because it is not something that you feel is important will simply remove one factor that might help influence the motivational climate. It will make achieving what you want just a little more difficult. At worst, it will also result in your being seen as uncaring. Similarly, what is important to you may not be to others. This is an important factor that any manager forgets at their peril. A further aspect of motivation now needs to be added, that concerned specifically with involving people.

INVOLVING PEOPLE

The word empowerment enjoyed a brief vogue in the mid-nineties, as one of a succession of management fads that would, if you believe the hype, solve all problems and guarantee to put any organisation on the road to success. If only. On the other hand there is sense in the idea of involvement which is essentially the meaning of empowerment.

TIP

Involvement may not solve everything, but it is useful and it does provide additional bite to the prevailing motivational feeling.

Empowerment in action

Rather than describe leaden definitions, let us start with an example. The Ritz-Carlton have enjoyed good publicity not only for the undoubted quality of their many hotels, but for a particular policy they operate. Say you are staying in one of their hotels and have (perish the thought) something to complain about. So, reeling from the stench from your mini-bar or whatever, you stick your head out of your room door into the corridor and take up the matter with a passing chambermaid.

Whoever you were to speak to the procedure would be the same. *Every* single member of the hotel's staff is briefed to be able to handle your complaint. They do not have to find a supervisor, check with the manager or thumb through the rulebook. They sort it. As they think fit. And they have a budget to do so – every single member of staff can spend so many dollars (it started as something like $500, but has no doubt changed) instantly, and without any checks, to satisfy a guest's complaint.

So, to continue our example, if the mini bar was dirty they could summon someone to clean it at once (even if that meant paying overtime), refill it with complimentary drinks and throw in a free bottle of fine wine and a bowl of fruit on a side table to make up to the guest for the inconvenience.

Such staff are certainly empowered.

It is an approach that gets things done. It regards staff as a key resource, not only to get tasks completed but who can, in many ways, decide just how they get it done. The empowerment approach goes way beyond simple delegation and plays on the appeal of responsibility to the individual to get things done and done right. It works in part because staff like it – being empowered is motivational.

Behind empowerment

On the other hand, empowerment does not allow managers to abrogate their responsibility, nor does it represent anarchy, a free-for-all where anything goes. The chambermaid (mentioned above) does not have the right to do just anything, only to select, or invent, something that will meet the customer's needs and which does not cost more than the budget to implement.

Staying with our hotel example, consider what must lie in the background, staff must:

◆ *Understand guests*, their expectations and their likely reaction to difficulties (and how that might be compounded by circumstances – having to check out quickly to catch a flight, for example).

◆ *Be proficient at handling complaints* so as to deal with anything that might occur promptly, politely and efficiently.

◆ *Have in mind typical solutions* and be able to improvise to produce better or more appropriate solutions to match the customer situation.

◆ *Know the system*, what cost limit exists, what documentation needs completing afterwards, who needs to be communicated with etc.

The systems – rules – aspect is, however, minimal. There is no need for forms to be filled in in advance, no hierarchy of supervisors to be checked with, most of what must happen is left to the discretion of the individual members of staff.

The essence of such empowerment is a combination of self-sufficiency based on a solid foundation of training and management practices that ensure that staff will be able to do the right thing.

Letting go

Often on training courses the room is full of managers tied, as if by an umbilical cord, to their mobile telephones or pagers. Many of the calls that are made in the breaks are not responses to messages, they are just to 'see everything is all right'. Are such calls, or the vast majority of them, really necessary?

The opposite of this situation is more instructive. See if this rings a bell. You get back to the office after a gap (a business trip, holiday, whatever). Everything seems to be in order. When you examine some of the things that have been done you find that your view is that staff have made exactly the right decisions, yet . . . you know that *if you had been in the office, they would have asked you about some of the issues involved.* Some of the time staff empower themselves, and when they do, what they do is very often right.

All empowerment does is put this kind of process on a formal footing. It creates more self-reliant staff, able to consider what to do, make appropriate decisions and execute the necessary action successfully.

Perhaps we should all allow this to happen more often and more easily.

Making empowerment possible

NOTE

Empowerment cannot be seen as an isolated process. It is difficult to view it other than as an integral part of the overall management process.

You can only set out to create a feeling of empowerment by utilising a range of other specific management processes to that end, though the process perhaps starts with attitude and communication. What degree of autonomy do your staff feel you allow them? If they feel restricted and, at worst, under control every moment of the day they will tend to perform less well. Allowing such feeling is certainly a good way to stifle initiative and creativity.

So you need to let it be known that you expect a high degree of self-sufficiency, and manage in a way that makes it possible. All sorts of things contribute, but the following – all aspects of communication – are certainly key:

◆ *Clear policy:* empowerment will only ever work if everyone understands the intentions of the organisation (or department), their role (clear job descriptions) so as to allow them to put any action they may need to decide upon in context. The other requirement of an empowered group is an absence of detailed rules to be followed slavishly, but clear guidelines about the results to be aimed at.

◆ *Clarity of communication:* this has been mentioned before, but is especially important in the context of motivation. Any organisation can easily be stifled by lack of, or lack of clarity in, communication; an empowered group is doubly affected by this failing.

◆ *Little interference:* management must set things up so that people can be self-sufficient, and then keep largely clear. Developing the habit of taking the initiative is quickly stifled if staff know nothing they do will be able to be completed without endless checks (mostly, they will feel, made just at the wrong moment).

◆ *Consultation:* a management style in which consultation is inherent acts as the best foundation for an empowered way of operating. It means that the framework within which people take responsibility is not simply wished, perhaps seemingly unthinkingly, upon them, but is some-thing they helped define – and of which they have taken ownership.

◆ *Feedback:* empowerment needs to maintain itself, actions taken must not sink into a rut and cease to be appropriate because time has passed and no one has considered the implications of change. Feedback may only be a manifestation of consultation, but some controls are also necessary. Certainly the overall ethos must be one of dynamism, continuing to search for better and better ways to do things as a response to external changes in a dynamic, and competitive, world.

◆ *Development:* it is axiomatic that if people are to be empowered, they must be competent to execute the tasks required of them and do so well. Remember too that useful development is itself always a significant motivator.

An enlightened attitude to development is motivational. A well-trained team of people are better able to be empowered, they have the confidence and the skills. An empowered and competent team is more likely to produce better productivity and performance. It is a virtuous circle.

At the end of the day the answer is in your hands. Keep too tight a rein on people and they will no doubt perform, but they may lack the enthusiasm to excel.

TIP

Management should have nothing less than excellence of performance as its aim.

Market pressures mean any other view risks the organisation being vulnerable to events and competitive action.

On the other hand, too little control, an abrogation of responsibility and control, also creates risk. In this case staff will fly off at a tangent, losing sight of their objectives and, at worst, doing no more than what takes their fancy.

Like so much else a balance is necessary. Empowerment is not a panacea, but an element of this philosophy can enhance the performance of most teams. Achievement and responsibility rank high as positive motivators, and empowerment embodies both. Motivation will always remain a matter of detail, with management seeking to obtain the most powerful cumulative impact from the sum total of their actions, while keeping the time and cost of so doing within sensible bounds.

Empowerment is one more arrow in the armoury of potential techniques available to you, but it is an important one. Incorporate it in what becomes the right mix of ideas and methods for you, your organisation and people, make it clear to people how you operate and it can help make the whole team work effectively.

The following ten keys to achieving/adopting a motivational style summarise what makes for success:

1. Always think about the people aspects of everything.
2. Keep a list of possible motivational actions, large and small, in mind.
3. Monitor the 'motivational temperature' regularly.
4. See the process as continuous and cumulative.
5. Ring the changes in terms of method to maintain interest.
6. Do not be censorious about what motivates others, either positively or negatively.
7. Beware of panaceas and easy options.
8. Make sufficient time for it.
9. Evaluate what works best within your group.
10. Remember that, in part at least, there should be a 'fun' aspect to work.

TIP

Make motivating, and the communication that transmits it, a habit.

Take a creative approach to it and you may be surprised by what you can achieve with it. The motivation for you to motivate others is in the results.

AIMING FOR EXCELLENCE

Finally in this chapter, remember that even the best performance can often be improved.

NOTE

Motivation is not simply about ensuring that what should happen happens. It is about striving for – and achieving – excellence.

All sorts of things contribute, from the original calibre of the staff you recruit to the training you give them, but motivation may be the final spur that creates exceptional performance where there would otherwise only be satisfactory performance.

It is an effect worth seeking; and it is one multiplied by the number of staff involved. How much more can be achieved by ten, 20 or more people all trying just that bit harder, than can be by one manager, however well intentioned, doing a bit more themselves?

Motivation makes a real difference.

6

Taking Responsibility for Communication

Communicate (v.) 1. (tr.) transmit or pass on by speaking or writing, pass on, impart (feelings etc) non-verbally (communicated his/her affection) 2 (intr.) Succeed in conveying information, evoking understanding etc. 3 (intr.) Share a feeling or understanding.

What is communication? Silly question? The *Oxford Dictionary* defines communicating as 'transmitting or passing on by speaking or writing' and 'succeeding in conveying information, evoking understanding'. It seems straightforward enough in theory but in fact it is fraught with dangers, many of which are hidden. Communication is not just speaking or indeed writing. Something else has to occur for the communication to be complete. There has to be a recipient and the recipient has to engage in the communication too. Both sides need to take responsibility for the communication.

MAKING AN IMPACT
Studies have proved what perhaps we all know: that we

make our first impression on someone very quickly and that first impressions last.

You have 0–15 seconds to create a first impression.

The studies show that we have a maximum of three minutes before someone has made a firm assessment of us. It is said that some people even make their initial decisions, form opinions or judgements about people within 0–15 seconds. This may even be with people that you have not yet been formally introduced to or have shaken hands with. People are reluctant to reassess us. The tendency is to look for evidence that the first impression was correct and ignore any evidence that it was incorrect.

People will make more decisions about you and you about them through the initial impact you create. They may not consciously realise what it is, yet they will have developed a belief, judgement or attitude about you based on the overall impact of the first meeting (telephone meetings included).

So the impact we make in the first moments of meeting someone will determine how that person perceives us, assesses us and what that person expects from us for a long time afterwards. We may not like it, but this is the way we work. The impact we make is based on the three elements discussed below.

1. **What we say (the words)**. We may wish to be judged on the words we use and the ideas behind them but the studies

suggest that this accounts for as little as 7% of the impact we make. Much of this 7% comes from:

♦ The type of words we use (common ones are best, although language and vocabulary relevant to both individuals can be used).

♦ The type of sentences we use (short, direct ones are best).

♦ The way we phrase them (positively expressed ideas are more likely to be acted upon than negatively expressed ones).

2. **How we say it (the music)**. The nature of our voices has a much greater impact – studies suggest 38% of the impression we make comes from tone, volume, inflection, pitch and accent. If these qualities of your voice are consistent with what you say, your message will have a more powerful impact.

3. **How we look and move (the dance)**. The biggest source of impact, put at 55% (the latest studies seem to indicate as much as 80%!), is our physical and visual presence, conveyed by posture, facial expression, gestures, clothes, grooming and eye contact. It is astonishing how much is read into the nature of a person's handshake. If your visual impact supports what you are saying and how you are saying it, the impact you make will be powerful. If the impact is whole, consistent and integrated it is much easier for the other person or people to read and understand you. If 1, 2 and 3 are out of kilter then you will be sending out mixed messages, leading to confusion and misunderstanding.

An exercise on impact

How do I think I currently come across?

....

....

How do I actually come across?

....

....

How would I like to come across?

....

....

NOTE

Remember: the words, the music and the dance.

Planning how to make the impact

When you next give a presentation or a brief, work through the following questions.

1. What specific impact would I like to have?
2. What content will convey that impact – in terms of words and structure?
3. Describe the kind of voice that will convey the impact I want.
4. Describe the visual presence which will convey the impact. Think of dress, eye contact, physical contact, movements and expressions.

A final word on impact. The significance of the opening moments is not confined to the first meeting. Your impact on your colleagues in the first moments after you arrive at work will lead them to form conclusions about the mood you are in that day. Their behaviour thereafter will usually be based on the assumption that their conclusions are correct. Likewise, the impact you have when you walk into your home will set the atmosphere at home for the rest of the day.

> **NOTE**
>
> Every single thing you say and do has an impact.

Remember that our overall impact is represented by:

◆ visual aspects   55%

◆ the way we say what we say   38%

◆ words or the content of your message   7%.

So in order to remain conscious of our ability to influence other people, we need to know what particular body language or voice cues increase our ability to do this and how we can alter these cues if we are not getting the response we want.

'*A master communicator is a flexible communicator, ready and able to change their voice, body language state, feelings and attitudes in a moment.*'

IMPACT AND COMMUNICATION

Every single thing you say and do has an impact. The impact that you think you make may differ from the impression you actually make. Both of these may also differ from the impression that you want to make.

So to recap, your impact is made up of:

1. **What you say**.

◆ The words, ideas and structure of your message.

◆ Commonly used words in short, direct sentences have the most powerful impact.

◆ Long words in long sentences are difficult to follow.

◆ Jargon can be used when appropriate, particularly if used with other rapport skills.

◆ Positively expressed ideas are more likely to be acted on than those expressed negatively.

2. **How you say it**.

◆ Your voice conveys meaning by tone, inflection, volume and pitch.

◆ If these aspects of your voice are consistent with the content of what you say, your message will be more powerful and more likely to be understood in the way that you mean it.

◆ If what you are saying and the way you are saying it are out of kilter the effect can be quite the reverse:

misunderstandings and arguments will often result. Remember: deliver a congruent message.

3. **How you look**.

◆ Your physical presence conveys meaning through your posture, your expression, your gestures and movements.

◆ If these support your message the impact is very strong.

◆ If these undermine or contradict your message your audience will be confused and may misunderstand you.

Before any communication ask yourself: what impact do I want to have?

When all three elements (content, sound and visual) convey the same meaning you will have stacked the odds very much in favour of having your message understood.

The voice
What are the components of vocal communication?

◆ tone

◆ pitch

◆ volume/projection

◆ timbre/resonance

◆ tempo

◆ inflection

◆ emphasis

◆ vias (see below).

The voice is an instrument. And just as with any musical instrument it is flexible. For example – liken it to a wind instrument, the sound projected is dependent on the force of air passing through the instrument, and the shape of the outlet through which the air/sound is emitted.

It's not what you say it's the way that you say it!

If your words say 'This is the most exciting product developed this decade' and your vocal behaviour is flat intonation, lazy diction, low volume and energy, the listener will not believe you. Your vocal behaviour speaks louder than your words.

NOTE

Remember: deliver a congruent message.

Negative emotions are conveyed through intonation, which follows the pattern above, i.e. nervousness when closing for instance or dealing with objections. We may not even be aware these are taking place. (See below.)

To disguise these feelings or vias and achieve your objective, maintain an even tone, with equal emphasis on each word, and have the pitch dip down on the last syllable.

Negative communication habits or vias

Vias are the habitual and unconscious messages that contradict the verbal content of our communication. They are conveyed through vocal tones and inflections, body postures and gestures. They are a substitute for direct and effective communication. If you look at the dictionary definition of the word via, it means 'by way of'.

They usually surface when we are fearful or nervous of a situation, unhappy, angry, stressed, defensive, tired or blaming something or somebody. It seems that they literally pull themselves up out of the unconscious part of our selves in reaction to a situation or feeling. Normally, they have a negative effect on the person to whom they are being expressed. This person may not be happy with what they see or hear, because the tone of voice, facial gesture or body language conveys mixed or additional messages. All of this will amount to something incongruence.

Congruence – sounding and looking like you mean what you say

It is important to deliver one single message to your listener. We all learn at an early age how to convey more than one message in our voice. For example: one of the easiest ways to put another person down is to pay them a compliment in a sarcastic tone of voice: 'well I must say you look very nice today'. However, sometimes these tones can creep into our voice just when we least want them to. The mismatch of content, tone of voice and body language is one of the most common causes of misunderstandings, rows and arguments. In your private life you can often recover from these situations. In business you might create a disaster!

For example, there are many ways of saying 'Good morning'. You can come across as bored, irritated, disinterested, even sarcastic – or friendly, warm and approachable – depending on the way you say it. Your voice often reflects your mood, so check your mood and ask yourself what mood is appropriate given what you want to achieve.

You are more likely to achieve the outcome you want if you sound like you mean what you are saying. For instance, on all visits it is always appropriate to sound interested, friendly, confident and professional even when responding to problems or complaints. If you sound bored or sarcastic with a client who has a genuine grievance, you will anger them even more.

Exercise
Using positive langauge

1. Write down a list of words and/or phrases that sound positive, dynamic and would enable a client to respond positively in conversation.

2. Write down a list of words and/or phrases which sound negative, defensive and would deter the client from behaving positively in conversation with you.

Examples of positive dynamic professional language

Endeavour

How would you feel about this

Taking into account

High calibre

Flawless track record

I'm aware/conscious of

Elaborate

Something to build on

I see what you mean

How we could fit this

Benefit statements

This is what I'm going to do

My belief is that

In your opinion

I'll do my utmost

What I suggest is

What I can do is

We can work together

It's important for me that . . .

This/it enables me to . . .

I'll look into that

I have an idea of the best way forward

Would it work for you if we?

If you were in my shoes what would you do?

I may not have made this clear when I explained it to you

How does that sound

Given what you have said

I can work within these guidelines

Proven results

Experience speaks for itself

I've done my research/I've discovered that

Expand

Is there anything else I can do to help?

Alliance/liaise/mutual

What we can offer

I think/feel/believe

The best route/option forward

What's your feeling about this?

How would that suit you?

What I'd like to do is

I suggest/I recommend

I understand/appreciate/realise/respect

I'll get started on this right away

Partnership

Certainly

I've considered

How about we tackle it this way?

Use of language styles

Empathy: *'intellectual or emotional identification with another person.'*

You cannot know a man until you have walked in his moccasins
– *Native American saying.*

Or to put it in layman's terms, getting on the other person's wavelength, or putting yourself in someone else's shoes. Everyone may subscribe to the notion of getting on another person's wavelength, but how can we actively demonstrate empathy in a practical sense? Here is a simple checklist of actions that will help you to get on the client's side and them onto your side:

◆ Listen to what they have to say and acknowledge their ideas – especially if you don't like or agree with what they are saying.

◆ Find out what the common ground is between you.

◆ Be aware that you are talking to another human being. If face to face, remember eye contact.

◆ Be yourself – be authentic and real.

◆ Communicate in an assertive manner. Get into the habit of expressing ideas positively. The same piece of information expressed two different ways will have two different impacts. For example: 'I understand what the problem is here. Let's find a way of rectifying this.' As opposed to 'I hear what you're saying, but I don't think I can help.'

Words and phrases to enhance empathy and acknowledge the other person are:

◆ certainly

◆ how can I help you?

◆ thank you for that information

◆ how can we tackle this so you are entirely satisfied?

◆ is there anything else I can do to help?

◆ I realise

◆ I appreciate

◆ I understand

◆ I respect

◆ I see what you mean

◆ I'll be delighted to . . .

Assertion: '*A positive statement or declaration.*'
The aim of assertive communication is to satisfy the needs and wants of both parties involved; for example, the client's and yours. Assertive people tend to stand up for themselves in ways that do not violate another person. You will most easily achieve this, even in an awkward situation, by making positive statements, in honest, direct and appropriate ways.

For example:

- I think or I feel
- what I'd like to do is/what I can do is
- yes, I can do that for you
- I can help you with that/I know how I can help you
- I'll look into that for you/I'll check this information for you
- I suggest or I recommend
- I'll pass this on to the right department/person
- I'll get to grips with this immediately.

State what you want:

- I need to have the following information
- I'd like to get started on that right away
- I'll give this my full attention.

Distinguish between fact and opinion:

- how I see it is . . .
- my belief is that . . .
- the facts are that . . .

Ask straight, open questions to get the other person involved:

◆ what do you think?

◆ how does that sound to you?

If you have some feedback of a more negative nature to give, state the facts and tackle specific actions, not the person's attitude. Explain it in a way that is not accusing:

◆ I may not have made this clear when I explained it to you

◆ next time when you . . . I suggest you . . .

◆ there are a variety of ways to work with this.

Make suggestions that allow the other person to make up their own mind:

◆ supposing we tackled it this way . . . ?

◆ would it work for you if we . . . ?

◆ which option is best for you?

◆ what route would you prefer?

◆ have I missed out anything you consider to be important?

Aggressive communication
On the other hand, the aim of aggressive behaviour is quite different. It is usually to prove our superiority, to threaten, or to defend against what we perceive as a threat. People here tend to express their thoughts, feelings and beliefs in unsuitable and inappropriate ways, even though they may honestly believe their views to be right.

Another method of aggressive communication is to give a contradictory message in our voice, for instance by adopting a sarcastic tone: 'I see. So you're saying that I've been given the wrong information.'

Non-assertive or submissive communication
The aim of non-assertive communication tends to be to avoid conflict at all costs and hopefully to please others. People here fail to stand up for themselves, or attempt to do so in a way that can easily be disregarded. They tend to express their thoughts, feelings or beliefs in apologetic, cautious or self-effacing ways. Unfortunately this mode usually manages to please nobody!

Vague communication
This form of communication presents itself as unhelpful and vague.

Remember

◆ no vias

◆ congruence – saying what you mean and meaning what you say

◆ we leak the truth from every pore, so be authentic!

USE OF ENERGY
Energy creates enthusiasm. Having an appropriate level of energy can create confidence, assertiveness, warmth and for that matter anything we want it to as long as we know how.

Enthusiasm is one of the most powerful states that influences people in presentations. Your emotional state will influence their feelings about your service as much as anything you will ever say, as long as you are able to maintain rapport.

A state of enthusiasm creates a more energetic performance. Consider how we can create enthusiasm and energy by changing our physiology.

NOTE

Remember: we leak the truth from every pore, so be authentic.

Body language

Effective communication means meeting the needs of the recipient. One way you can judge his or her current need is to study their body language.

Body language is one of those areas where a little knowledge is a dangerous thing. You may have heard, for example, that people who cross their arms are being defensive, but they may cross their arms because it is comfortable, because they are cold, because that is their habit or because they want a cigarette and they find crossing their arms eases the craving. To reach any firm conclusions about body language you need to find several consistent signs – either several consistent signs from one person or from several people.

Body language can be split into two areas:

(a) the body language that you are responsible for portraying and modelling – your impact

(b) the body language you see displayed in another – other's impact on you.

We need to look for:

◆ *Clusters*. Several bits of body language that fit together to tell the same story.

◆ *Changes*. Changes in body language give a picture of how your message is being received.

◆ *Incongruence*. A mismatch between the words, the tone and the body language.

Positive indicators	Negative indicators
Open shoulders	Folded or crossed arms
Relaxed posture	Head-shaking
Nodding	Finger-pointing
Standing upright	Foot-tapping or moving feet
Smiling	Turning away
Gestures to describe or indicate	Swaying from side to side
Leaning towards	No eye contact/staring or frowning
Open-hand gestures	Hands behind head or back
Making contact with all the audience	Hunching shoulders
Eye contact	Tense/clenched gestures
Interested facial gestures	Clock-watching
Still feet	Stretching or yawning
Open posture	Twiddling or repeatedly touching hair

Excessive arm-waving
Fiddling with clothes
Looking at floor or other spot

If, or while, you are talking, you notice most people are looking at you with an interested expression, nodding and smiling at the right times and with an alert and open posture, carry on with what you are doing. Do not overlook the obvious – but do not try to apply theories unless you have the professional training to apply them.

Common things to look for:

◆ *falling asleep may mean*:
  —late night
  natural body rhythm after a heavy lunch
  —windows need to be opened
  —you're becoming boring.

◆ *fidgeting may mean*:
  —you're a boring presenter
  —we've lost track
  —can we have a natural break
  —can we get onto something more relevant.

◆ *shaking of heads may mean*:
  —I want to say something, but I won't
  —I don't agree with you
  —you haven't understood our needs.
  —you've blown it

Stay alert. If many people are looking away from you, appear bored or are fidgeting, you are losing them. If they looked very 'turned off' you may as well stop talking but if you have more to say, here are some tips:

◆ Say 'to summarise' and then give a brief summary of what you have said so far.

◆ Say 'what I still have to say covers' and then indicate what you have left.

◆ Increase the energy, pace or volume of your voice.

◆ Regain eye contact.

◆ Be critical of yourself – are you going on too long or repeating yourself?

◆ Finish what you have to say as concisely as you can.

◆ Create a situation to bring in audience participation or expression of views – use questions.

LISTENING SKILLS

Most people are not good listeners. We tend to be more interested in what we have to say, or what the couple on the next table are saying. We may have grown up with parents and teachers who in most cases modelled a poor standard of listening. Listening fully is hard work, demanding concentration and an acceptance of the other person's message unconditionally, even when we do not like what they are saying. We may even believe that to listen to others is a risk as it may be seen as weak.

Poor listening damages relationships and so adds cost to a business and to personal relationships. Good listening builds relationships, avoids misunderstandings and the errors that result from them. Good listening saves time and often results in the listener being listened to in turn.

The behaviours of a good listener are easy to identify. A person who is listening to another keeps a comfortable level of eye contact, has an open and relaxed but alert pose, faces the speaker and responds to what is being said with appropriate expressions, asks follow-up questions and offers encouragement such as a nod and a smile.

Two essential skills of listening, which are not so easily recognised because they are not usually part of everyday conversation, are:

◆ reflecting and

◆ **summarising**.

Reflecting means repeating back a key word or phrase the speaker has just used, or reflecting back the unspoken message that went with it, for example, 'You seem frustrated by this.' Reflecting acknowledges what the other person has said, shows you have listened and understood and so encourages them to say more. Reflecting is used a great deal by counsellors and coaches.

Summarising means reflecting back a summary of what the speaker has been saying. It shows you have listened and so builds rapport, gives the speaker a chance to add to or correct your understanding and acts as a milestone in the conversation, from which you can move on.

TIP

Allow people the dignity of being heard.

Adopting the behaviours of a good listener will help you but the real difference can only come from the self-discipline of a listening attitude – a genuine desire to take on board all that the speaker has to say. Suspend judgement, analysis, interpretation, rejection and postpone saying your bit, until you are sure you have fully understood what you will be replying to.

'A good listener is not only popular everywhere but after a while, he or she knows something.'

No one will listen to someone who is not listening to him or her. Remember to listen and let the other person know you have heard by repeating the key points they say.

If you listen, you will be able to do the following successfully:

◆ enable the other person to feel understood

◆ gain cooperation from them

◆ answer questions accurately

◆ make sure you have the correct information

◆ deal with complaints and difficult people

◆ retain control even if you don't know the answer

◆ ensure the other person feels special

◆ retain the attention and interest of the listener

◆ achieve the communication process

Some listening skills guidelines
What to do:

1. Give full attention to the person speaking.
2. Separate facts from opinion.
3. Identify key points and relate them to your existing knowledge.
4. Be rational.
5. Make appropriate eye contact.

What not to do:

1. Be thinking up counter arguments before the speaker has made a point.
2. Interrupt unnecessarily.
3. React emotionally.
4. Opt out when the subject becomes dull or complex.
5. Reject the content because the delivery is poor or there is a language barrier.
6. Succumb to distractions.

Duplication

Understanding and becoming conscious of duplication and how it happens will make you a better listener than you previously thought possible. Duplication is a natural process, it takes place in your head. What happens is that a person says something, then in your head you repeat it (rather like an automatic little voice).

The next thing that happens is your conditioning takes over. If you happen to like or agree with the idea, this is the point when you could probably repeat it word perfect. If you don't like it, disagree with it, or even feel criticised, you will automatically react in a negative way or defend yourself. This idea is, very simply, an opinion or viewpoint of another.

However, what human beings do is have their own ideas waiting, ready to be thrown in at the first opportunity. Thus, these will be the only things they have their attention on at that moment. Listening, sadly, is forgotten. Therefore, if you treat duplication as the ability to hear someone's idea completely, and intact, you can call yourself a good listener.

Exercise

This set of exercises will enhance your ability to listen to information without the need for judgement, inter-pretation or interruption. Do this exercise with a partner. Your partner reads out the sentences and you duplicate them – not interpret them but duplicate exactly what has been said. No cheating!

Simple

1. Our computer is broken, can you fix it?
2. I am very sleepy, I can't stay awake.
3. This lighting is harsh, I can't work under these conditions.
4. I really don't like public transport, it's uncomfortable and inconvenient.
5. He's often late and it really irritates me.
6. Next Monday we will advertise; be prepared for the response.
7. I don't understand what you want, could you explain it again?
8. Thanks a lot for your help. I really appreciate it.
9. Clients don't really have time to listen to long explanations.
10. This week we have to prepare for a visit by the managing director.

Medium

1. My team does not follow my instructions, so many things are left undone.
2. Could you give this report in by Wednesday? One copy for me and one for the department manager.
3. It is so difficult to get clients to understand our position. How can we explain ourselves more easily?
4. It was reported in a recent magazine that we spend 80% of our time producing only 20% of our results.
5. Client service is the ability to give the client what he wants, when he wants it and at a price he can afford.
6. They are a very professional company; all of the staff seem experienced and on the ball.
7. The thing that impressed me was their energy, enthusiasm and commitment to helping their clients.

8. I find using this computer much easier now that I have been trained; everything seems clear and makes more sense.
9. She is great to work with; her communication is so clear I always feel motivated and confident.
10. If you could do anything you want, would you complete the Iron Man Triathlon in Honolulu?

Advanced
1. We judge ourselves by what we feel capable of doing, while others judge us by what we have already done.
2. Appreciation is a wonderful thing; it makes what is excellent in others belong to us as well.
3. Our attitudes control our lives; attitudes are a secret power working 24 hours a day, for good or bad.
4. I am not discouraged because every wrong attempt discarded is another step forward.
5. The essence of leadership is to listen, learn, understand, evaluate, decide and communicate.
6. The art of being taught is the art of discovery, as the art of teaching is the art of assisting discovery to take place.
7. If you tell me I may listen. If you show me I may understand. If you involve me I will learn.
8. You can make more friends in two months by becoming really interested in other people than you can in two years trying to get other people interested in you.
9. There are two ways of meeting difficulties: you alter the difficulties or you alter yourself to meet them.
10. Fear nothing, for every renewed effort raises all former failures into lessons, all sins into experience.

DIRECTING A COMMUNICATION

Can you recall times when you have either been speaking to somebody on the phone or you have been at a friend's house? You look at your watch and say, 'Wow! Is that the time? I must have been talking to you for ages!'

This usually happens when the two people concerned are giving each other space in their conversation. There is a feeling of ease, ideas are being passed to and fro, a natural exchange. Some may call it rapport.

This is true; however, what is most probably happening is that some essential communication points are being addressed. You are each directing the conversation to get the information you want from it and allowing the other person to share their viewpoint. In other words a balance of listening and talking. There are times when you will want to find out some information, or ask a question of somebody and you will not get back what you have intended.

Often, people deliver a line of communication without a supporting question. Immediately, there is a break in conversation that someone has to pick up. If you are in a service situation and your role is one of being the information provider, it would make sense that to find out information you would need to ask questions. A statement is not a question.

There are usually two reasons for this. Most people at some stage fall into one of two camps: they either ask a lot of questions, 'the Spanish Inquisition' type, or they give away too much, 'the lots of information' type. If you can remember moments when you have been on the end of these, you will know how infuriating or boring it was and how much you may have wanted to get away.

People like either to ask a lot of questions and then never listen to your answers, or they never ask a direct question in case they get a negative reply. Therefore they never get the information they want with which subsequently to direct a successful conversation. They then lose control and the other person takes over. They also do not verbally or physically acknowledge the other person; that means the recipient will feel that they are not being heard. This, if not noticed, can lead to potential breakdown in the conversation.

Avoid answering a question with a question. Always acknowledge what the other person has said.

Directing a communication cycle
To direct the communication, use this formula:

1. Begin the conversation by introducing yourself and giving away some personal information. This is called the *inform stage*.
2. Once you have given away some information, ask a direct question of your listener/client. This is called the *invite stage*.
3. *Wait* for a response.
4. On receiving this, 'duplicate', in other words *listen* – to every word!
5. *Acknowledge* and, if necessary, *repeat* the essence of their response. When you are finding out facts and figures, you may find it useful to repeat everything word perfect.

6. If they have given you some unsolicited information, use this to *move to the next stage*, e.g. your question: 'How satisfied have you been with the service of the agencies that have provided you with contractors in the past?' They respond: 'Not very, because they haven't contacted us since the contractors began.'

7. It is best here to *put yourself in the picture*. Using 'I' followed by your idea is usually a self-disclosure. It informs them about you, making the conversation a bit more personal and then puts you back in the driving seat, ready to ask another related question (invite a response).

8. If at this point you do not have the opportunity to ask another question, nine times out of ten they have begun to direct the conversation. Remember, it is you who wants the information.

The steps above become easier with practice. It may help to sum them up in one phrase:

◆ **inform/invite.**

Three types of questions that can be used to direct a communication:

Closed
Designed to elicit precise information, often in the form of a single word. Commonly, the person answering will expand on the information given in the form of a justification, e.g. 'Can you give me suggestions as to how agency working relationships can be enhanced?'

Directed
Designed to guide the discussion along a route that advances the conversation in some way advantageous to you, e.g. 'Now you have told me how you like to work in partnership with an agency, can we identify something more concrete for the way forward?'

Open
Designed to give the client a chance to talk. Open questions use trigger words such as: who, what, where, why, when, which and how. 'How do you currently monitor the agencies who work with you?' 'What qualities do you look for in an agency?'

PRESENTATION SKILLS AWARENESS

◆ **Presence** – the way the voice and body language are used.

◆ **Relating** – the way rapport is used.

◆ **Questioning** – matching the question to the situation.

◆ **Listening** – listening for everything.

◆ **Positioning** – telling the story the client's way.

◆ **Checking** – gauging the client reaction as you go.

Presentation skills – what to look/listen for
Opening the meeting

◆ Adjusting to the room – seating of clients.

◆ Exchange of business cards and brochures.

- Knowledge and ability with presentation aids.

- Recapping previous conversations.

- Thanking the client for their time.

- Asking the client about time.

- Checking their preference for type of presentation.

- Adjust mentally to presentation before beginning.

- Assertive body posturing e.g handshake/eye contact.

During the meeting

- Checking the audience is with you.

- Looking for positive/negative cues and signs.

- What to do when the presentation is not going your way.

- Use open, closed, checking and verifying questions.

- Clarify information.

Closing the meeting

- End positively.

- Review next steps.

- Who does what and by when.

Selling features and benefits

- Awareness of matching these to client needs.

- Knowledge.

◆ Knowing the brands and their USPs (unique selling points).

Handling client objections

◆ Ability to listen.

◆ Ability to debate persuasively.

◆ Acknowledgement.

◆ Weaving features and benefits as a way of handling objections.

Communication skills

◆ Clear ideas.

◆ Good use of tone, volume, pitch and pace.

◆ Use of pause.

◆ Warmth and openness/authenticity.

◆ Professionalism.

◆ Asking questions.

◆ Acknowledgement.

◆ Creating and inviting involvement.

Rapport skills/matching

◆ Voice.

◆ Tone.

◆ Pace.

Awareness of body language/matching and mirroring

◆ Eye contact.

◆ Hand movements.

◆ Posture.

The mind – personal barriers and how to overcome them

Whenever you set a goal or have an objective to achieve, a presentation to deliver or a potentially awkward conversation with your clients, it is inevitable that somewhere along the road to achieving it, you will hit a barrier.

A barrier consists of three dimensions:

◆ emotions

◆ body sensations

◆ thoughts.

The emotions you experience when hitting a barrier will be one or a selection of the following:

◆ apathy

◆ grief

◆ fear

◆ anger

◆ pride.

You will probably be able to identify the emotion(s) and accompanying thoughts that you experience in the pursuit of your objectives when you are under stress.

TIP

Positive affirmations work: 'I can do this.'

Negative emotions are a product of the mind, originally designed to ensure your survival, i.e. fear. These emotions have been blown up out of proportion by modern day values, resulting in similar body sensations being experienced in potentially embarrassing situations as in life threatening ones. They must be overcome in order to communicate constructively. Your response to these feelings determines your ability. Your desire to be right, i.e 'I can't do this because' perpetuates them. To shift these emotions requires a shift in perspective. Be honest with yourself about the source of the problem and be willing to change your mind regarding the issue.

Remember that all negative emotions stem from a fear of something or someone.

How to deal with barriers:

1. Acknowledge to yourself that you have hit a barrier.
2. Check off your emotions, body sensations and thoughts.
3. Communicate to your clients in a positive, empathic or powerful way, or tune in to a colleague for some support.
4. Review your original goal for this visit and be flexible – you don't have to be right.

5. Do not procrastinate. Head for the challenge. You will experience satisfaction.

Conquering nerves

People often fear their nerves will get the better of them – this sometimes becomes a self-fulfilling prophecy. Two things to remember: nervousness usually shows far less than you think and some nervousness is necessary to help you give your best.

TIP

Preparation saves perspiration!

Below are some tips for overcoming anxiety. Most of them have already been mentioned:

+ Name the fear – explore exactly what it is you are scared of. When you do this you often find it is nothing to be scared of at all.

◆ Take a few slow, deep breaths. Smile. Lower your shoulders.

◆ Have an image in your mind of a time or place when you were relaxed. Bring this image to mind before you start.

◆ Make sure you pause. Your recipient(s) need(s) those pauses and you can enjoy them too.

◆ Get to know some people from your audience, if in a presentation or meeting.

◆ Remember, most people want you to do well.

◆ Slow down!

◆ For presentations, follow the guidelines on notes, rehearsals, preparation and so on.

◆ Replace negative thoughts with positive ones: 'I can't do this. I know I'll fluff it. I can feel my voice going already!' Override this downward spiral with a positive one. 'I'm ready for this. They are on my side. My voice is strong. I'll stun them!'

Visualise this: You are saying your final sentence. Your communication/presentation has gone perfectly. Your final point comes out loudly and powerfully. Everyone is agreed on a satisfying course of action. Your audience/recipient(s) smiles warmly.

You have succeeded!

Written communication

The thing to remember about written communication, whatever form it might take, is that the recipient cannot see you or hear you. Therefore they have no option but to accept what they read. So we must pay particular attention to that fact and consider how the recipient is going to read (in both senses of the word) what we have written. The rules are simple:

◆ put yourself in the shoes of the recipient

◆ say what you mean

◆ avoid jargon

◆ keep it simple

◆ make it easy to read and understand (layout is important)

◆ avoid innuendo, sarcasm, *double entendre* and ambiguity

◆ stick to the point and answer their questions.

Electronic mail

Email is, to my mind, not an excuse for shortcuts and abbreviations that the reader may not understand (a silly example but one that caused me a lot of trouble was when I received an email that said: 'C U 7.30 pm.' I interpreted that as 'see you at 7.30 pm.' What the sender meant was 'curtain up at 7.30 pm.' Needless to say, I missed the show!). Email is also not an excuse for what I call dumping: getting on your soap box and rambling on and on. And last but not least, it is no reason for avoiding face-to-face conversation.

NOTE

Remember: keep communication simple and straightforward.

(7)

Change Management

Change (changj) (v.t.) to alter or make a difference; to put one thing for another; to shift; to quit one state for another; to exchange.

Management (n.) the act of managing; administration; body of directors controlling a business. Manage (man'naj) (v.t.) to direct; to control by use of the hands; to carry on; to cope with; (v.i.) to direct affairs; to succeed.

A mystique has grown up around the process of change and its management. As a result, if not handled correctly, fear and resistance suddenly abound at the prospect of it. For many, titles like 'interim management' consultants specialising in 'change and transitional management' send a cold shiver down the spine, up the cynical ratio attitude of others and set tongues clicking with censure throughout.

With all the advances of life, communication and global connection we have been able to carry forward into the 21st century, having an understanding and working with the speed of change is a skill that is often neglected.

> **TIP**
>
> To be successful in business today means that you have to be
> fluent in change.

Whether you are taking advantage of new opportunities big
or small, like facing a takeover bid, working in conjunction
with others on a particular job, or simply changing software
and systems in the office, you need to be prepared for the
process. Plan a time schedule to follow, factor in periods of
assessment and recalibration.

*It is change, continuing change, inevitable change, that is the
dominant factor in society today.*

Isaac Asimov

Being fluent in the process of change empowers people to
be willing to try out in w scenarios and make choices and
decisions with less fear. It is possible to learn how to manage
change so that you too can become fluent in the process. The
first thing to understand is that change occurs constantly in
our personal and professional lives. We live with change
every day of our lives, and accept the process very often
without conscious thought.

In this chapter we review:

◆ *Recognising the need for change* – change is ubiquitous.

◆ *Taking the positive view* – coping with change.

◆ *Managing the progress of projects* – facilitate the change.

RECOGNISING THE NEED FOR CHANGE

Change is ubiquitous. There are many reasons for change in the workplace. Some are dramatic for the organisation as a whole, from boardroom level through to the most junior support staff. For example:

♦ Mergers and acquisitions and new leadership.

♦ New company strategy.

♦ Downturns in the company's business to respond to internal or external influences.

♦ Enforced changes of company culture to react to new legal or marketplace influences i.e. staff retention.

Smaller scale of changes such as:

♦ Introduction of updated technology.

♦ A review of sales and marketing collaboration.

♦ Development in the life cycle of a product or service.

♦ Control measures to monitor and reduce costs.

There are two factors that cause change and affect the way we are willing to work with the process:

(1) Change caused by external influences that are beyond our control. For example, an external influence that the British know well – the weather. Another example is organisational change caused by business PESTs – political, economic, social or technology change. We try

to forecast and pre-empt them, but mainly we react to them.

(2) Internal influences that we usually have some degree of control over. For example, your career. If you are unhappy at work you can think about changing your job. You can plan for leaving and go through the various stages towards your goal. You have a personal motivation to find the energy to go through the process of change and cope with the additional stress while still working full-time in employment. You have control; you can assess and recalibrate any thoughts or decisions through the transition of change. You are managing your own change.

The only unchangable certainty is that nothing is unchangeable or certain.

John F. Kennedy

There is a third dimension to change. On occasions we take steps on trust that it is the right action. We have faith in the person managing the issue for us, even if we do not understand the complexities of it. We will do our part by asking all the questions we need to in order to have faith and trust that it is the right action to take. For example, we decide the best ways forward in our careers to give our families the life we want now and desire in the future by setting up a series of financial structures designed by advisers that we understand in principle. We will follow the advice of others when they show us a high level of understanding and knowledge of their industry in relation to our situations. We trust them and make sure that we give whatever it is they need to make the process happen. We 'buy in' to the concept and are personally motivated to be a part of the process. We are proactive in our behaviour; we have control, can assess our progress and change focus if needed.

When managers achieve the 'buy-in' of the whole team, they have inspired the personal motivation of each team member.

This motivation and energy is the currency needed to manage the process of change in the workplace, and you as the manager need to know how to make it happen. Your team need to trust you and have faith in you, and you need to have the same in them.

But still, even with so much naturally accepted change in our lives there can be an unconscious wariness and fear of change in the workplace. When this becomes a prevalent attitude it will create barriers, increase difficult situations and be destructive to the process of change management.

Key words:
fear of change versus **authenticity** in the workplace
change for change's sake versus **benefit** of change in the workplace.

Whatever the catalyst for the change and the scale of the change, the business sector – the company – has human beings at its centre. The company is only as good as its staff and how successfully the changes are implemented is down to the relationships within the company.

TAKING A POSITIVE VIEW

Coping with change. We have looked at the necessity to recognise that change is a normal part of life. To manage its progress means getting everyone involved using their own personal motivation to create a sustainable energy in the business.

The three Cs to successful change management and transition:

◆ *communication = value*

◆ *cooperation = action*

◆ *cohesion = embrace*

(1) Communication = value

When changes are viewed as negative, either by the workforce as a whole or individually, automatic conscious and unconscious barriers are raised. These barriers can act out in a variety of forms, from aggressive voluble behaviour, to passive aggressive action revealing itself in non-cooperative behaviour. Either way the role of the manager is to get the team to work together by consulting their expertise and experience.

When you blame others, you give up your power to change.

Douglas Noel Adams

Gone are the days of successful bosses having all the answers. The company as a whole needs to trust and value each others' input and concerns. A team who view the proposed changes as directed from the top, in a way that is beyond their control to influence, produces a reactive, fear-based group. Fear and distrust are expensive commodities in the 21st century business. Decisions need to taken by people who are empowered and courageous enough to accept change as a normal part of life and to bring the process of transition to a successful conclusion. That may mean changing the way things have been done before, or constant assessment and recalibration of current situations.

Either way, managers need the 'buy-in' of everyone. That means, to make management simple *recognise people need to be able to align their personal values to the changes and allow them to give you the benefit of their expertise and knowledge to gain the best and most efficient ways of achieving it.* They will be driven by a personal motivation to give their best, be innovative and creative.

Key words:
External influences **beyond** personal control and valued input = **reaction and fear**.
Internal influences **within** personal control and valued input = **proactive behaviour and fearless motivation**.

What kind of change manager are you?
First read this account. The board of a company decided that as part of their modernisation and long-term strategy they needed to change the packaging logistics of a major product. In order to achieve this they needed to transport a liquid product across a road, from one side of their factory to the other side.

The board commissioned architects and consultants to apply to the local planning department to build a bridge to transport the product. It appeared to be the best solution to the senior managers. Their application was refused. They spent many more hours and money studying the original building plans to see what alternatives there could be. Still, further proposed applications were refused. The board and consultants were stuck. The whole ethos of the company felt threatened as the location of the factory and its warehouses were as much a part of the product as the product itself.

TIP

Successful change management requires a culture that encourages everyone to know their knowledge and expertise is valued -- whatever their status in the organisation may be.

One morning, the chairman of the board was driving to work, and saw ahead of him the caretaker on the side of the road. The man disappeared into the building but by the time the chairman passed that spot he saw to his amazement the caretaker standing on the other side of the road. The chairman stopped his car and shouted to the caretaker 'How did you do that? Get from one side of this road to the other without walking across?'

Answer? There was an underground maintenance passage. For some reason it was not on the building sites plans, but it was in daily use by a small section of the workforce.

Moral: Never be too proud to ask or underestimate the knowledge and experience of every single person you employ.

Key words:
Communicate with everyone = show you **value** their contributions, **gain** from their experience and improve your business **bottom line**.

Now let's look at your strengths and weaknesses as a manager in relation to the process of change.

Patrick Forsyth in *Communicating With Your Staff* lists the characteristics of the 'ideal manager' people want. One of the most important is 'working for someone I learn from'. Managing the process of change, whether all-encompassing or on a much smaller scale, provides an excellent, positive opportunity learning.

Listed overleaf are other characteristics. Work through the exercise and assess how you are perceived and what skills you may need to aid the process of change management.

Exercise

Informal management appraisal feedback process

The following exercise is designed as your own managerial SWOT test – strengths, weaknesses, opportunities and threats. Complete one copy yourself then read the instructions below.

Mark yourself from 1 as the lowest to 10 as the highest.

◆ Do I give positive learning experiences?

◆ Am I fair/consistent/honest?

◆ Do I give time to people/listen?

◆ Am I a good communicator?

◆ Am I able to understand others' points of view/see the broader picture?

◆ Can I deal with matters promptly/delegate/challenge?

◆ Am I trusting/respectful?

Give a blank copy of this list to at least one other person who you know will be truthful, honest and not afraid to 'say it as it is'. Ask them to mark you from 1 (the lowest) to 10 (the highest). Thank them for their time and support to do this task for you *whatever the result*!

The truthful, fearless feedback and information you receive from this exercise will help you identify your strengths, give you direction in skills you need to refresh or learn and highlight areas that you may have to delegate to others to ensure a positive outcome of your change management.

That is joined up management – management made simple.

Whatever the reason for change, and regardless of the degree of the effects within the organisation, change needs to be viewed as a positive action and you need to get everyone to give their continued best performance, even if they personally do not agree with the aims and objectives.

TIP

The benefits of managers knowing the workforce across the organisation are innumerable and surprising.

How do you get everyone on side, find their personal motivation, rise above negative attitudes and uncooperative behaviour? Feeling dizzy just at the thought? Here comes the second of the three C's for successful change management and transition.

(2) Cooperation = action for change

For full cooperation to be recognised within a company it is helpful to break down its structure into three interconnected parts to see the different directions of viewpoints.

◆ *Personal* – individual employees.

◆ *Team/department* – groups with their own structure of reporting and support role within the company.

◆ *Organisation* – the board, the bosses, stakeholders, the intangible whole.

Each of these three separate parts need to work together even though they often come from differing viewpoints. A cost-cutting measure in the accounts department may mean a change of job description or extra workload to an employee. The boss's idea of better customer relations by installing new systems could mean early retirement to a loyal employee because that member of staff feels they are 'too old to learn new tricks'. What company knowledge will you lose when the employee retires? Remember the caretaker's knowledge in the factory. Alternatively, a bright young member of staff who spots an opportunity that is in an unheard of area or age group known to the company might be thought, by the older boss, to be too risky a venture. Each of these three parts that make up companies are fundamentally real, live, feeling and thinking human beings. The organisation as a whole has a responsibility to the individual, and the individual has responsibility to the organisation, through their department and personally. Together, all pulling in the same direction they can work SMART.

S – specific
M – measurable
A – achievable
R – realistic
T – time-tied.

Treat people as if they were what they ought to be and you help them to become what they are capable of being.

Goethe

Motivation
Individual employee reactions to the changes are based on their own personal interests, values and attitudes. Even the most loyal and tireless employee will, sooner or later, view the end goal and transition for change from their

own perspectives. As outlined in Chapter 5, in the 1950s Abraham Maslow introduced the concept that there was a hierarchy of needs, and that as each need was met, people's aspirations move up to the next stage. If their needs are not met, they are not motivated. To recap, this hierarchy of needs is:

1. Food and water – (pay).
2. Shelter/safety – (housing).
3. Belonging – (community).
4. Esteem from others – (prestige).
5. Self-esteem – (empowerment).
6. Self-actualisation – (values and meaning). The highest aspiration.

Conversely, until each level of need is met, people cannot move on to the next stage.

Recalling the list of Maslow's hierarchy of needs it is clear that the process of change within a company could upset some of the aspirations and motivations of the workforce faced with merger and acquisitions. For example, this change could bring a different company culture so the issues of realigning values and meaning, feelings of empowerment and prestige are brought in to question. Furthermore, a sense of community within the staff will be disturbed, along with the underlying worries of job redundancies, bringing the most basic concerns of not being able to provide safety, shelter, food and drink.

If you put good people in bad systems you get bad results.
Stephen Covey

A large part of a smooth transition of change management is to be able to motivate your staff to work alongside you, giving you their best, even though part of the process may challenge their own needs.

Here are some ways you may hear people's worries and frustrations being voiced:

- What effect will it have on my quality of life?

- Does it make the job more, or less, challenging?

- Is the new challenge interesting and a great learning experience or just another word for work overload?

- How does it affect my career prospects?

- Do our 'leaders' know what they are talking about?

Depending on personal viewpoints, however sound the change may be from a business point of view, it is these opinions that will decide the barriers to change, not to mention damaging morale through office gossip around the coffee machine if the management choose not to properly brief the work force.

Key words:
Professional **imposed** needs = personal **demotivation**. **Personal needs** = professional **motivation** and **excellence**.

Exercise

Referring to Maslow's hierarchy of needs, these questions should be answered twice. First, ask yourself, to gain your own perspective. Second, ask the relevant people involved in the change.

1. What are the aims and objectives of this process of change?
2. What do I know and feel this change will mean to my team and their working life?
3. What will these changes mean personally to them?
4. What needs to be done to manage this change?
5. What support do we need as a team?
6. What support do we need individually?

This exercise will help you to focus on what needs to be done and how to do it. It also forms a framework for you to measure the degree that you and your team are in alignment. Now you need to decide who is going to be responsible for which tasks, and agree a time and date to meet again as a team to report back on progress, discuss further ideas and concerns.

MANAGING THE PROGRESS OF PROJECTS

Accountability and responsibility

Management of loose ends

It is often forgotten that before you can be seen to start the process of change, you need to have a closure of the 'pre-change culture/system'. Change is perceived as the way forward to a better state of affairs for the business. The clarity of change message, the benefits, timings and a structure to work through are usually carefully planned, looking forward.

Here is a tale of looking forward and loose ends. A media company was deciding to update their central pool of mobile phones and portable IT equipment. These were given out to members of staff and freelancers so that they were able to carry out their jobs 'in the field'. All the equipment was the same. No member of staff had their own customised equipment and it was part of the company's strategy to keep control of the costs of a potentially expensive, but essential, area of their business. As time passed, new equipment was essential. The company had started from a small, intimate base. There was a basic system of recording who had what equipment, but more often than not it was a trust system of cooperation.

As the company was becoming successful, and employed more staff and freelancers, this informal system was no longer working. The department responsible could not get a senior manager to 'sponsor' their concerns as the excitement escalated with the thought of the new whizzy kit.

Individual commitment to a group effort – that is what makes a team work, a company work, a society work, a civilization work.

Vincent Lombardi

The 'company' thought that the problem was to update and change the equipment. No one, except those working closely with the problem, realised that a new system of tracking staff loan of equipment was needed whatever the state of the equipment. It was not until the new kit started to go missing that the bosses realised they had not tied up a loose end.

Moral: Change management needs to look back to complete the past, and then move on in the future.

Exercise

◆ What management of loose ends and closure needs to happen before we can move forward through a successful transition of change?

◆ Who will be responsible to see the closure through?

◆ What is the time schedule we need?

Here comes the third of the three Cs for successful change management and transition.

(3) Cohesion = embrace change

Part of the process of change management is to work through the project as a cohesive group. Rarely – unless you are a one-man-band – does only one person have to do all the changing on their own.

Group dynamics

A snappy way to remember the dynamic process of working on a project with a group is to think of the following five words – forming, norming, storming, performing, mourning.

◆ *Forming* – the group has to get together and agree the way forward. Often there is a uniting cause or goal that binds the team that starts the process of cohesion.

◆ *Norming* – when the group have agreed the ways forward and resolved the structure of working together they begin a working relationship.

◆ *Storming* – as the group settles down to the task, differing opinions, styles and ways of working become apparent and friction appears. This needs to be addressed.

◆ *Performing* – as this working relationship matures, and everyone in the team has trust and faith in each other, and the team as a whole, they perform at their best.

◆ *Mourning* – this fifth step is often forgotten, but when a process of change comes to an end, the goal has been achieved, there is a sense of relief, but in some cases of change management, anti-climax and loss. For example, if the change has meant redundancies or relocation there is a physical process of ending rather than the celebration of a job well done.

Exercise

Where are we in the transition of change management?

◆ forming

◆ storming

◆ norming

◆ performing

◆ mourning.

Keep this exercise close at hand to review where you are. If a new person enters the team, or other factors relating to the project suddenly appear, you may have to re-form, norming and storming again to get to the performing at best level.

Different styles and personality types
There are many models and analyses of different styles and personality types found within the business world, e.g. Meyer Briggs, Belbins, DISC. They create a language to describe 'how we act' or our behaviour. Research has shown that characteristics can be grouped together into differing styles. For example DISC:

D = dominance – challenge
I = influence – contacts
S = steadiness – consistency
C = compliance – constraints

Everyone is a mixture to some degree, but usually they display an overriding disposition to one style.

Here follows a brief look at how you might recognise people by these four styles.

◆ *High Ds* – love change and will change the status quo. They will reinvent the old way focusing on one goal – results. They rock the boat in their quest for results and will find more efficient ways to get the job done. Their high emotion is anger/short fuse.

♦ *High Is* – may not notice change but are natural mediators, not liking conflict. They can verbally persuade both sides to come to an agreement. Part of this is due to their ability to focus on the bright side of the issues. People like them, and 'buy' their concepts and ideas.

♦ *High Ss* – do not like change and need much preparation. Once involved in the planning process they are a great asset. Often goals are set and the plans to achieve them are not thought out well. They can bring lofty ideas back into the realm of the real world and point out the gaps and flaws in the plan due to their logical thinking process.

♦ *High Cs* – are concerned by the effects of change. They are great objective thinkers and task orientated. Their sceptical nature looks at all the possibilities before they buy into the plan, but being allowed to use their natural talents they are a great asset to a team to carry through the plan. They collect data, and are always analysing, testing and clarifying.

Having read through those basic style types, you will understand that different people will work best and embrace the process at different stages of the change management process. They will also react to the process of change in contradictory ways to each other. You will need to assess the people you are managing and use their best attribute to aid you.

Support and development for change managment
Listed below are different ways that you can find support for yourself and others through the process of managing change.

It is only as we develop others that we permanently succeed.

Harvey S. Firestone

Internal: *Mentoring* is industry specific. Often thought of as process of 'elders' supporting and advising the juniors in their career path. With the process of change, there now is 'reverse mentoring', a system where the youngsters with, for example, knowledge of new technology at their fingertips will mentor their 'elders' to learn and understand new innovations.

Buddy system is a way of giving people within a team the support they need when it is not possible to consult the group as a whole. Buddying creates a system where peers can consult, discuss and decide on issues that crop up, and find ways of resolution, rather than calling the whole team together and wasting the valuable time of meetings. *Coming together to find solutions to a problem rather than just presenting the problem for concenus.*

External: *Executive coaching* – either one-to-one or in teams. A professionally trained coach works with the client to identify their personal motivation to give their best at work. The coach works with the person as a whole, including personal attitudes and circumstances as well as professional concerns and aspirations.

TIP

Personal needs drive professional performance.

SUMMARY

◆ Change is part of life.

◆ Recognise personal needs, values and motivations within the company.

◆ Consult to gain from everyone's company knowledge, experience and expertise.

◆ Ask for and give support.

◆ Manage the ongoing change process by reassessing and calibrating along the way.

Enjoy the process of change management!

8

Defusing Difficulties

Defuse (v.tr.) 1. remove the fuse from (an explosive device) 2 reduce the tension or potential danger (in a crisis, difficulty etc).

Misunderstandings can easily occur in our communication with others. More often than not when there is a breakdown in communication it has something to do with the past. We will frequently blame the breakdown on the other person. However – and this is a hard lesson to learn – if we are really honest with ourselves we will be able to see that it was probably something to do with the way we communicated that caused the misunderstanding.

Communication is the successful transmission of an idea from one person's mind to another person's mind. It is a process fraught with obstacles.

◆ First, the communicator has to translate the ideas into some medium, such as words. Most of us have difficulty with this at some time. The communicator also has to overcome any internal barriers to communication.

◆ Next, the medium has to carry the communication to the

recipient. All sorts of problems can occur here: words get drowned out.

◆ Then the communication has to be received. All kinds of filters and distortions can creep in here. The recipient:
  – may not be concentrating
  – may have prejudices about the communicator
  – or have made assumptions about the message.

◆ The recipient may not like the communicator and if the recipient wants to misinterpret what he or she is receiving, they will.

◆ Finally, the words have to reproduce the original idea. As we have different ways of thinking, the idea will have different impacts and interpretations for different people.

Looking at this tortuous route, it is not surprising that communication goes wrong so often. One study showed that, on average, people leaving an hour-long business meeting had three to four major misconceptions about what had been agreed.

Usually, we find it hard to acknowledge we have hit an internal barrier. So we invent reasons and excuses for ourselves through a process called **rationalisation**. We convince ourselves that the problem does not lie within us – that would be too hard to bear – so we rationalise, find reasons why the problem must be external.

THE ROOTS OF INTERNAL BARRIERS
Delving into the roots of internal barriers to effective behaviour takes us into the world of psychology. Work-

place psychology has a poor reputation, partly because of the jargon it attracts, partly because untrained people dabble in it and partly because dismissing it as 'soft stuff' or 'pink and fluffy' is a defence from the need to examine one's psychology.

In her popular and readable book *Feel the Fear and Do It Anyway*, Susan Jeffers argues that internal barriers stem from a fundamental fear of 'I can't cope' in certain situations. So we go to great lengths to avoid these situations and cover up our fear. Will Schutz goes further: in books such as *The Truth Option* he explores the basic components of what people fear they cannot cope with. He, like other writers, suggests three dimensions to the fears that drive us:

◆ *If, deep down, I feel I am not a very significant person*, I fear being ignored because that confirms my feeling and I could not cope with it. So I will avoid situations where I might be ignored.

◆ *If, deep down, I feel I am not a very competent person*, I fear being humiliated because that confirms my feeling and I could not cope with it. So I will avoid situations where I might be humiliated.

◆ *If, deep down, I feel I am not a very likeable person*, I fear being rejected because that confirms my feelings and I could not cope with it. So I avoid situations where I might be rejected. For example, it is this fear that often prevents people giving negative feedback or constructive criticism.

'Success comes in cans not in cant's.' – Anon

We all have each of these fears to some extent but usually one leads the others. Do not waste time speculating on the basic fears of other people you interact with; this can be fun but it is always speculation, even when you have been fully trained in these ideas. Take responsibility for your own fears and deal with those first.

Beliefs – the door to excellence

Attitude – the key ingredient
What is attitude? An attitude represents both an orientation towards or away from some object, concept, or situation and a readiness to respond in a predetermined manner to these. Both orientation and readiness to respond have emotional and intellectual aspects and they may, in part, be un-conscious.

'*I do not like thee, Dr Full, the reason why I cannot tell!*'

'*A settled and often permanent disposition or reaction to a person or thing.*'

Our attitudes and beliefs are very much based on life's experiences. Many of our beliefs and attitudes remain in our unconscious mind and we act out of them mechanically.

The critical factor to consider about our attitude is whether it is positive or negative. Having a positive mental attitude is much more than thinking up glossy slogans and the like, it is an orientation to living, a way of living and relating to the world. In this way our attitudes control our lives and almost always, the attitude and behaviour of the people with whom we come into contact (see Attitude Cycle).

Attitudes are a secret power working 24 hours a day, for good or bad. It is important that we know how to harness and control them. Success or failure is primarily the result of the attitude of the individual. *A change of attitude can bring about an outstanding change of results.*

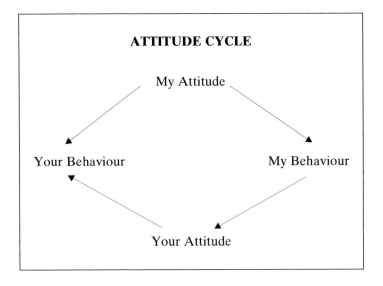

ATTITUDE CYCLE

My Attitude

Your Behaviour   My Behaviour

Your Attitude

You will find the most successful people are deeply motivated towards their goals and objectives in life. You won't usually find successful individuals who have become successful by doing what they hate or dislike in life.

'Give me a man of average ability and a burning desire and I will give you a winner in return every time.'

A. Carnegie.

Attitudes are often generated from our accumulation of beliefs. We desire what we value, and what we value is a reflection of our attitude and beliefs.

Beliefs

Belief delivers a direct command to your nervous system. When you believe something is true, you literally go into the state of it being true. Handled effectively, beliefs can be the most powerful forces for creating good in your life. On the other hand, beliefs that limit your actions and thoughts can be as devastating as resourceful beliefs can be empowering. Beliefs are the compass and maps that guide us towards our goals and give us the surety that we will get there.

The question is what kind of beliefs are the most useful to have and how do we develop them?

The creation of excellence begins with our awareness that our beliefs are a *choice*. One of the biggest misconceptions people have is that beliefs are a static intellectual concept. Our strategies for survival are generated through our life experiences and observations.

> *'They can because they think they can.'*
>
> Virgil.

So what are beliefs? They are pre-formed, pre-organised approaches to perception that filter our communication to ourselves in a consistent manner.

Where do we get our beliefs?

1. From the environment. If all you see is failure, if all you see is despair, it's very hard for you to form the internal representations that will foster success.
2. Events, small or large, can help foster belief. There are certain events in everyone's life that they will never forget.
3. Belief fostered through knowledge. Direct experience is one form of knowledge. Another way is through reading, seeing movies or viewing the world as it is portrayed by others.
4. From creating results in the past. The best way to create a belief that you can do something is to do it once. If you succeed once, it is far easier to form the belief that you will succeed again.
5. Establishing beliefs through creating in your mind the experience you want in the future as if it were here now. In other words experiencing results in advance.

Most of us form our beliefs haphazardly. We soak things up – good and bad – from the world around us. The key is to become aware that you are not just a leaf in the wind. You can manage and control your beliefs and therefore consciously direct your life and behaviour.

The event/decision pattern

Event Something happens.

Decision A negative outcome is decided upon, ie: 'I'm not going to get what I want.'

Actions Subsequent actions are tinged by the decision, which will affect your voice, tone and behaviour which can appear to make your decision look like the truth.

Right The result or outcome is then a self-fulfilling prophecy. You were right!

In order to reverse the process to a positive outcome, observe the decisions you make. You will know when you have made a negative decision when, no matter how hard you try, things still keep going wrong and you find yourself in a never-ending downward spiral.

Identify the decision, remake it into a positive outcome in line with your desire and then consciously apply actions in line with that outcome (voice tone, facial expression, physical behaviour).

The outcome will then be one of satisfaction as opposed to one of being right.

HANDLING QUESTIONS, OBJECTIONS AND AWKWARD SITUATIONS

We experience the above every day and in many different forms. Sometimes it is because the person has a genuine problem. Other times, it is because they don't understand some information or because of an emotional reaction that has no logic or reason behind it.

NOTE

Remember: usually when there is a breakdown it has something to do with the past.

These problems, challenges or difficult situations are usually genuine for the person in their predicament. The challenge occurs when the receiver of the communication perceives it to be negative. The purpose here is to stay calm and detached from the emotional response, thereby hearing exactly what is being said. Otherwise any of the above can be received as an attack. As a result they become things to be feared, guarded against or, preferably, avoided altogether.

The common and habitual reaction to being confronted by these is to defend yourself, by attacking, changing or ignoring the idea you are receiving. This makes it difficult to resolve the problem and cooperation is therefore almost impossible. In essence there are two things happening.

◆ There are the words of the complaint/problem.

◆ There is the emotional charge attached to the complaint/problem.

The words will usually imply an unfulfilled need, want or expectation and would have to be satisfied before the communication can proceed. The emotional charge simply has to be heard and understood.

It is important to remember that someone you consider a difficult person is usually delivering a group of ideas that you either don't like, agree with or know what to do with. If you remember this when you are met with a difficult situation, you will increase the chance of a mutually satisfying result.

In a situation where the automatic reaction is to defend, remember to:

(a) Pay attention, listen, duplicate and understand.
(b) Make no assumptions.
(c) Listen for any free information.
(d) Acknowledge their ideas, repeating the essence if necessary.
(e) Respond to them by informing with an action or solution.
(f) Ask a question to ensure the situation is clear or satisfactory – if not identify the expectations before completing the meeting.

Never over-explain, defend, make excuses or ignore their point of view. Empathise, rather than sympathise.

All they want to know is:

(a) That you fully understand their problem.
(b) What you are going to do about it.

If you deal with people in this way, every situation of this kind should result in both parties being satisfied. This may look impossible. This result is not dependent on the situation being totally resolved, it is however dependent on your ability to respond and be responsible in your communication.

In summary the cycle of actions is as follows:

◆ Keep your voice pitch and tone low and evenly paced – match where possible.

◆ Duplicate the essence of the problem back to the other person.

◆ Tell them their options and what you can do to the best of your ability.

◆ Follow through on any actions you agree to take as a result of the communication.

◆ If this is a situation that you found hard to handle, tell someone about it and express any residual feelings immediately.

◆ Do not make promises that you may not be able to keep.

Additional tips for handling difficult situations

Handling anger
Let them express their anger. Anger is usually a short-term emotion. Unless it is allowed to dissipate it will accumulate and fester. Someone who is allowed to vent their anger will be more cooperative later on. The key to this is to listen and acknowledge the emotion until it is fully released. You may get stored-up anger from other things that are nothing to do with the complaint, question or criticism. Again, do not take

this personally. They will probably be eternally grateful for being allowed to get a lot of other things off their chest!

Gently take back control. Once you have heard the complaint, tell them that you would like to help solve the problem and that you will do everything that you can within your responsibility to do so.

Take notes. Focus on the issue and the possible solutions, not the emotions.

TIP

Distinguish the facts from the story.

If the person is abusive, *gently repeat that you want to help.* Explain that you can do this better if they will tell you what they want. If appropriate, tell someone else about the situation, for instance a colleague or manager.

Some dos

◆ Show interest by calling the person by name and letting them know that you are listening.

◆ Show empathy. Imagine how you would feel in the same position. Draw on your own personal experiences of times when you have been confused, misunderstood or needed an answer or explanation.

◆ Restate the essence of the complaint fully so there are no misunderstandings. Make sure you understand the criticism, objection, request or need.

◆ Consider the possibility of human error. They may have misheard something. They may not have all the facts.

◆ Admit the problem. If there is one, apologise.

◆ Ask the client/person what they want. Offer alternative solutions, not just one.

◆ Take responsibility. Own the problem until it is resolved or passed on to the correct person to sort out.

◆ Identify time scales. If the problem cannot be sorted out immediately, tell the client/person how long it is likely to take, even if you think this may throw up another complaint.

Some don'ts

◆ Don't take it personally, even if you were responsible for the error. Commit to overcoming the problem as soon as possible without resentment or blame.

◆ Don't give a flat 'no' answer. As much as possible offer a short explanation as to why what is being asked is not possible.

◆ Don't assign blame. No one cares. They just want a solution, not a justification of the original error.

◆ Don't make promises. If you aren't sure you can deliver a promise do not make one. It will only disappoint them later on and damage the relationship even further.

◆ Don't lose your sense of humour, no matter what the complaint is.

A summary of handling objections

◆ objection

◆ listen/duplicate

◆ understand

◆ acknowledge (by clarifying or qualifying)

◆ inform (using features, benefits or USPs)

◆ ask questions

◆ satisfy objection

◆ agree to the next step.

Remember objections don't always come in the order you think that they will. Take each and every opportunity to listen and acknowledge. This is by far the best way to handle any objection.

THE ART OF CREATING RAPPORT

Effective and positive communication begins with recognition and appreciation that each of us is unique and different. It can be achieved by tuning in your body language, tonality and words to those of another individual, even if that individual seems to be the opposite of you.

All of the above is most definitely achievable, but the first step towards mastery of rapport and communication is to know what you want in any communication. Once you have this established you will need three skills to work with the process.

1. **Sensory acuity and awareness**. Become more alert and aware of the responses and actions of others. See more, hear more and feel more. This is a skill that can be learned.

2. **Flexibility**. If you are not getting the response you want, you need to be able to change your behaviour until you get your desired outcome. You cannot expect the other person or people to change.

NOTE

Use rapport to get on the same wavelength.

3. **Congruence or authenticity**. This simply means that what you say and how you say it convey the same message. Rapport or empathy is essential for establishing an atmosphere of trust, confidence and participation within which people can respond freely.

Communication seems to flow when two people are in rapport, their bodies as well as their words match each other.

What you say can create or destroy rapport but that accounts for only 7% of the communication. Body language and tonality are more important. People in rapport tend to mirror and match each other in posture, gesture and eye contact. Their body language is complementary.

Successful people create rapport and rapport creates trust. This is achieved by consciously refining your natural daily rapport skills. Through matching and mirroring body language and tonality you can very quickly gain rapport with almost anyone. This matching must be done sensitively and with respect at all times. Matching does not mean mimicry which is mostly considered offensive.

You can mirror and match:

◆ body postures and gestures

◆ head angles and movements

◆ voice tone, tempo, pitch, rhythm and volume.

There are just two limits to your ability to gain rapport: the degree to which you can perceive other people's postures, gestures and speech patterns and your skill in matching them in the dance of rapport.

Through doing these things sensitively, and with integrity, you build a bridge to another person's model of the world. Our inner world experience is made up of feelings, sounds and images, just like the outer one. We all differ in how we use our senses on the outside, so we will also differ in the way we think. Some people talk to themselves, others think more in pictures, others in feelings or sounds. We know what thinking is for ourselves and may assume it is the same for others. However, each person is unique and therefore different.

Our beliefs and interests also condition what we notice.

There are three main representational systems or modes through which people access, store and filter their experience. These are: *visual, auditory and kinesthetic*. We operate in all three modes at different times, but tend to have one preferred mode.

The skill in creating rapport is being aware of the other person's mode and flexible enough in your own language and behaviour that the visually oriented people can see what you are saying, auditory people can hear you loud and clear and the feeling (or kinesthetic) people will get to grips with your ideas.

The essential rapport skills

Awareness
This is essential if you are to control a communication. It enables you to:

◆ Identify the style of communication that is preferable to the other person.

◆ Understand accurately what he/she wants – not what you think they should want.

◆ Effectively manage and respond to potentially emotional situations.

◆ Observe the impact your communication is having and alter it accordingly.

Awareness is achieved through the use of the senses and is a skill one can learn. You literally learn to see hear and feel more.

Flexibility
'People like people who are like themselves.'

It is easy to talk with someone with whom you experience 'being on the same wavelength.' Flexibility enables you to alter your mode of communication to suit your client, 'to speak the same language'. This may mean going outside your comfort zone. Matching, mirroring and pacing are simple ways to create easy rapport, once you are flexible enough.

By using our communication skills we can defuse difficult situations and even turn them around. The **iceberg model of**

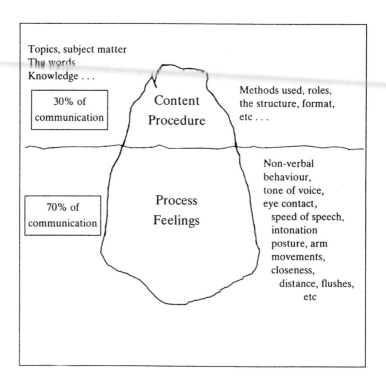

Topics, subject matter
The words
Knowledge . . .

30% of communication

Content
Procedure

Methods used, roles, the structure, format, etc . . .

70% of communication

Process
Feelings

Non-verbal behaviour, tone of voice, eye contact, speed of speech, intonation posture, arm movements, closeness, distance, flushes, etc

communication (page 192) illustrates the need to pay attention to what is going on below the waterline. Not responding appropriately to and dealing with people's feelings is often the cause of upset. As I said earlier, the processes and feelings below the waterline are embedded in the past and are therefore rarely anything to do with the issue at hand. Nevertheless, unless they are dealt with they will become the cause of the breakdown.

The iceberg model of communication

1. Communication demands 100% responsibility by all people involved if what is intended to be conveyed is to result in the desired outcomes.
2. When communicating, people must be aware of both their own personality and the personality of others.
3. The biggest failure is not responding appropriately to the **processes** and **feelings**, through insufficient attention or lack of personal development. Not surprisingly, the outcomes are less than 30% effective.

Resolving issues

The three major causes of breakdowns are withheld communications, broken agreements and unfulfilled expectations. Often it can be all three! Whichever one it is, until you can get to the bottom of it you will not be able to move the conversation on. The diagram overleaf illustrates the route you need to take in order to resolve the issue.

Delivering bad news

Nobody likes to be the one to deliver bad news. This can often be a case of 'don't shoot the messenger'. There isn't a great deal you can do if someone is hell bent on shooting the

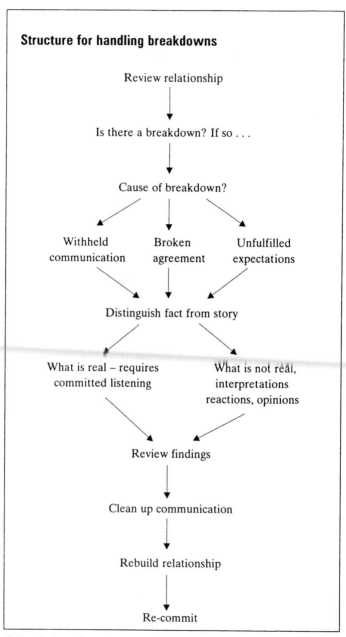

Structure for handling breakdowns

Review relationship

Is there a breakdown? If so . . .

Cause of breakdown?

Withheld communication | Broken agreement | Unfulfilled expectations

Distinguish fact from story

What is real – requires committed listening | What is not real, interpretations reactions, opinions

Review findings

Clean up communication

Rebuild relationship

Re-commit

© Four by Four Consultancy

messenger. You may feel bad about it but you must not take it personally. If you do, you will simply get into a negative spiral and end up with more upset to deal with – your own and the other person's. The guidelines here are much the same as before:

◆ empathise – put yourself in their shoes

◆ tell them the facts

◆ be sensitive to their feelings

◆ give them time for the news to sink in

◆ listen to them if they need to off-load

◆ offer your support

◆ end on a positive note.

In the case of redundancy or termination of employment, be absolutely crystal clear about the facts. Give people reasons and explanations, if you can, rather then justifications. In matters of discipline, be proactive. Make sure that people know the rules and the boundaries at the beginning of a contract of employment. If people are aware of the rules there is no excuse and it will make your job that much easier.

The final word on matters of employment is: get your facts straight. Consult a specialist in human resources or employment law. Warning: this is a minefield, proceed with caution. Many an employer has found himself or herself in court dealing with cases of unlawful dismissal. So seek professional advice and deal with it by the book.

9

Encouraging Creativity

Create (kre-at) (v.t.) to bring into existence out of nothing; to originate; to make; to produce; to give rise to; to cause; (Slang) to cause a commotion. –creation (kre-a-shun) (n.) the act of creating, esp. of bringing the world into being; the world; anything created; any original production of the human mind.

Creativity (n): the ability to create.

Creativity in business drives ideas and provides the platform for constant development and improvement to maximise overall performance.

The idea of creativity should not be confined to the creative industries, such as advertising, or part of a research and development team where the act of creativity is understood as a necessary function of the business, and is seen to have a direct effect on the company's profitability.

Managers in other fields often believe that creativity is a working practice that is irrelevant to them with little direct effect on their bottom line, let alone their team performance. What those managers are thinking about is an individual creativity. Visions of the mad R&D team leader spring to mind. Corporate creativity is not the same as individual creativity. The goal of creativity in the workplace is to make the act of creativity a normal part of everyday business life, that will reach across the company from product development to managerial development.

Any activity becomes creative when the doer cares about doing it right, or doing it better.

John Updike

The power of including creativity in the manager's skill base should not be underestimated and, on the whole, many managers practise some form of creativity while resolving daily issues on a subconscious level. The key to creative management is to make this process more successful, to identify strengths and develop areas of weakness.

The creative manager needs to sustain an open and creative environment where all team members have a forum for discussion of ideas without reprisals. Moreover, the creative manager should possess the courage to reassess current working methods and question the unthinkable whilst remaining realistic about the idea's development and implementation. One further point to bear in mind is that the creative manager must accept full responsibility for their decisions and be accountable for ongoing assessment during the development of a project.

TIP

Never underestimate the power of giving a few words of encouragement during a creative failure.

The business world is changing at a speed unknown to previous generations and, with the advent of the World Wide Web, email, e-commerce and m-commerce, business is now global.

Whether the business you manage is a one-man band or an FT 100 company, global events such as those on 11th September 2001 can affect you directly or indirectly. For example, a sudden plummet in exchange rates would exert an external influence over business that called for creative spontaneous strategies to counter adverse effects. However, creativity should also be proactively applied to the more controlled or routine tasks such as marketing plans, staff retention or implementation of EU legislation.

Every human being has an innate sense of creativity. Not to explore this conscious creativity within the workplace will cause problems in the longer term.

In this chapter we will review:

◆ *Building creativity into management* – sparking a creative culture.

◆ *Realising and driving ideas for excellence.*

◆ *Active team dynamics* – sustaining creative, alive collaborations.

BUILDING CREATIVITY INTO MANAGEMENT

Sparking a creative culture. In order to build creativity into management, there needs to be an atmosphere of openness, honesty and trustworthiness. Everyone has heard of the boss who sat at the head of the boardroom table and asked the team assembled to comment on a document he had written. 'Read it' he said waving the report in the air 'and then come back and tell me what I want to hear.' Ha, ha!

It would take a very brave person to step out of the line in this kind of environment and question or suggest further improvements. But what can be done and how can creative thinking help in a situation like this?

The role of the creative manager

There are two aspects to building creativity into the work-place. The first criterion is to encourage and maximise the personal creativity intrinsic to everyone. The second is to provide the environment to allow creativity to flourish.

> **TIP**
>
> You get the best out of others when you demonstrate trust and loyalty to them and give the best of yourself.

The role of the creative manager is to harness these energies and implement them to maximise the individual's and the collective's performance. The ever-increasing demands to better the economic, social and environmental working standards or 'triple bottom line' is yet another pressure on today's managers. Reassessing business productivity and profitability scenarios calls for creative thinking and creative management. In an aggressive business world it is the creative manager who will catch the proverbial worm.

Are you a creative manager?

Grade yourself between 1–5 (1 = poor, 5 = excellent) on each of the following questions

◆ Do you learn from your and other people's experiences?

◆ Do you look to improve your own performance?

◆ Do you encourage opinions and feedback from work colleagues?

How creative is your working environment?

◆ Does the company culture encourage open debate about working?

◆ Could mistakes from the past happen again?

◆ Does the workplace enable a healthy work/life balance to suit individuals' needs?

The perfect score for the truly creative manager would be 15 and for a creative environment would be 15. What can you do to ensure that you can achieve this? This scoring allows you to consciously assess your skill as a manager to use creativity and the environment in which you work.

Key skills of the creative manager

◆ Strive for genuine improvement

◆ Excellent interpersonal skills

◆ Courage to follow through and be accountable.

Case history

A large international consultancy, whose bread and butter it was to advise others, often forgot to look closer to home. Producing and arranging printing of their annual report had become a joke within the office. Much time and a huge amount of money had been wasted due to poor planning; diagrams and copy were forever changing leading to costly artwork being reproduced and the unbudgeted expense of typesetting the document again and again. For many years even when the run final signoff had taken place and printing had started, changes were made. As a number of departments were involved no manager actively took any responsibility to manage this project.

The factors later discovered to enable this to happen were:

◆ This was seen as a run of the mill, annual task that had to be done. No one was ever thanked for is completion and therefore there was no recognition for being responsible for it.

◆ No one really had time for the project. Managers were appraised on their clients' account work. Their involvement in the annual report was not considered to be a measure of their performance.

◆ It was thought that the level of managers involved in this project would cooperate in an informal way, as they knew each other so well.

Due to a restructure within the company a new manager came on board who was not shy about taking the reins. Using the skills of a creative manager he realised the need to improve this situation. He encouraged all those concerned to be open and honest about the difficulties and also what aspects had gone well. Creating a non-judgemental environment to reflect the pros-and-cons of the project management laid the foundations for developing and improving future cross-company projects.

It is not fair to ask others what you are unwilling to do yourself.

Eleanor Roosevelt

In this case using creative management skills identified the improvements needed for next year's annual report while the project was still fresh in everyone's mind, rather than brushing it under the carpet and hoping everyone would forget until the following year. This manager used excellent interpersonal skills and had the courage to voice concerns to make a genuine improvement for the company's benefit and all those involved. This was the company's annual report to stakeholders, investors, clients and prospective clients. The annual project was reinstated to be appreciated as the important document it was in its own right, rather than a necessary task.

Strategies to build on

You have now identified the level of your personal and environmental creativity. For development to take place here are some strategies to review to build upon to bring creativity into your management style and the workplace.

Example areas where a manager can exhibit creativity in the workplace are:

- *on a one-to-one basis with members of the team*

- *creativity meetings*

- *cross-company cooperation.*

One-to-one

A new manager working in the media was frustrated with his newly formed team that never voiced any opinion at meetings. Any points of action that were agreed never seemed to be followed through. Even though the team consisted of highly talented, hardworking people, somehow the objectives and goals got bogged down by fruitless discussion, other day-to-day tasks taking up all available time, and so on. All the members had been with the company for some time, but due to a restructure they were required to work closely together for the first time.

In answer to the manager's demands for help, he began one-to-one coaching to aid his professional management. To his surprise, these coaching sessions gave him an understanding of his performance, and skills to be able to work with each member of his team. He realised that everyone is different. In this case, both on a professional and personal level. The company restructure that had created his team had different impact on each member. The opportunity to him as a new manager also confirmed to another member of the team that she had reached the highest level she might ever be in the company. She felt passed over and consequently disengaged from anything but the essentials of his job. The manager also began to clarify what talents and skills he had already and which new skills he needed. He began to realise that any negativity in the team was not personal to him, but the situation. Sadly, however, he became the butt of discontent.

The manager started to work with each member of the team, allowing them to voice their concerns and, like him, assess what development was needed for each individual. The process also set the benchmark for the team expectations (see Chapter 7 – Change Management).

A creative manager takes the time to focus on individual team members' values, expertise and purpose to benefit the team as a whole.

◆ Value their strengths and expertise.

◆ Give them the accountability for their own job performance.

◆ Support them in the development of their skills and talents.

◆ Challenge them to work at their full potential.

◆ Provide an environment where their own creativity can flourish.

Creativity Meetings
Business meetings that do not encourage creativity tend to be analytical and judgemental. Often a decision has to be made there and then with little room for reconsideration. The pace of the meeting is rapid and serious with closed questions being asked. There is a narrowing of options in order to make a decision that is carried. Often the meeting style does not allow full participation of all members present.

Meetings that invite creativity tend to be non-judgemental. Open questions are asked around the table, there is a flow of ideas. It is relaxed, and there is a sense of fun. Any decisions that are made allow for a recalibration or expansion at a later date if needed. Everyone is expected to contribute to the discussion and is accountable for the follow-through of options and decisions agreed at that meeting.

When chairing a creativity meeting it is important to remember that all dialogue should actively be encouraged. Manager need to inspire and encourage inspiration from their team (see Chapter 2). Everyone should feel comfortable expressing his or her opinions, no matter how abstract, illogical or unrealistic. The first point of a creative meeting is to stimulate discussion. Conversation should be open and organic. The creative manager should recognise when closed questions are being asked and lead the conversation back to an open forum.

Without inspiration, the best powers of the mind remain dormant. They are the fuel to us which needs to be ignited with sparks.

Johann Gotfried von Herder

Examples of closed and open questions. Closed questions tend to be able to answered with a yes or no. They do not open up, or lead on the thinking while answering the question, eg:

◆ Is this an effective strategy for you?

To be asked this as an open question would inspire creative thinking thereby giving a full and more considered answer, eg:

◆ What makes this an effective strategy for you?

Turning this into an open question invites the answer to explore what is happening, leading on the thoughts to broaden the possibilities. By making questions open, externally voiced internal thoughts can be tested for their validity. Sometimes the explanation of the answer is interrupted by 'You know, while I was saying that to you I realised it isn't quite true . . .' That open question has opened up the exploration to find the reality and the best way forward. Not only does this give the questioner a more complete view but allows others attending the meeting to understand the complexities and arouses their own questions and thought processes.

Some other examples of closed and open questions:

◆ *Closed* – Have you finished your research yet?

◆ *Open* – If you had more time, where else would you research?

◆ *Closed* – It sounds like you are stuck between two choices – is that true?

◆ *Open* – I can see the two obvious choices, but what are the alternative less obvious options?

In order to build a creative meeting structure the following guidelines should be recognised by all those participating. As the manager, you will need to ensure that:

♦ However off the wall they may seem, all ideas need to be heard.

♦ There is no instant rejection of any ideas.

♦ Nobody's ideas are wrong. There is no point-scoring of 'my idea is better than yours'.

♦ Everyone around the table needs to be included.

♦ Use different techniques to spark up creative thoughts.

♦ Make it fun.

♦ If the meeting is to be time-defined, map out a time schedule with points when the ideas need to be pushed forward into accountable actions.

Cross-company cooperation

A creative manager not only works with people he or she is responsible for or to, but fosters relationships throughout the company and across all levels. The creative manager is interested in what is going on in the company as a whole and recognises the benefits in forming bridges across the company. By forming these informal relationships, it opens up the opportunities for shared information and future cooperation. Awareness of other departments' agendas and objectives offers a fresh view of working within the same environment.

No man is an island, entire of itself; every man is a piece of the Continent, a part of the man.

John Donne

It is worth bearing in mind that the departments that people may traditionally approach for a solution may not be the best source for answering a question. For example, an IT department may be responsible for software but a colleague in an entirely separate department may have gained years of practical experience in using the software and may be able to offer you a more creative and unconventional solution. Making that connection only comes about when managers and staff know each other. They all have the knowledge of who's who in the company and what their responsibilities are.

REALISING AND DRIVING IDEAS FOR EXCELLLENCE

Einstein suggested *Imagination is more important than knowledge*. And the creative manager?

As a manager you are responsible for achieving the objectives of your department. There is always a constant flow of areas to concentrate on, and there may be many reasons why you need to realise and drive ideas for excellence.

Whether you are a manager in the world of profit or the 'not for profit' sectors, there is the need to keep the standards of the workplace high and achieving the objectives that are the reason for your business's existence in the world.

To illustrate some of the big-picture business scenarios here are typical ways concerns are expressed by stakeholders:

◆ Do we compete with the 'new kids on the block' that are undercutting the customer price of our product?

◆ What should we do to make sure we don't lose our staffs' inherent knowledge of the company as it is being restructured?

◆ How do we create a 'triple bottom' line accountability and still be profitable? – economic responsibility, social responsibility and environmental responsibility.

Employees' personal concerns in relation to the business could be expressed in the following ways:

◆ If there is no money for training how can I learn the skills I need for my new position?

◆ Where do I get the support I need?

◆ How do I stop losing my team to competitors when 'they' offer so much more in pay and working conditions than we do?

But how can creative management help resolve issues such as these? Creative managers who fostered a level of communication and trust have in the past allowed the development of many innovations that have influenced our society today, and will continue in the future. For example, Hollywood studio executives believed television to be a six-month fad and Daryl F. Zanuck, head of 20th Century Fox, said 'People will soon get tired of staring at a plywood box every night'. In spite of the reservations of these 'experts' the development of television was completed and promoted. The impact on us of television is well understood today, and their technological advances continue to open up wider possibilities for use and influence on our lives.

NOTE

When the CERN Institute, Switzerland, originally created a better internal communication system, they did not know it would become the basis for the worldwide net, creating change and opportunities globally.

The manager's role is to make sure their teams run efficiently, and create the right environment to enable them to have the ideas to keep ahead. It is also the manager's responsibility to recognise the potential of zany, off-the-wall ideas and the possibilities of converting them into viable business initiatives.

To be able to allow creativity and capitalise on success, the manager needs to encourage experimentation and learn from experiences, to be able to tolerate a degree of failure within the team work and to see it not as a failure, but as a great idea that seemed in theory to work, but in reality did not.

Blocks to creative management

Too many cooks spoil the broth
It is more creative to bring the core members together, and then to be responsible for taking ideas to the peripheral

interested parties for their comments and suggestions separately to gain greater insight and benchmarking opportunities.

Pride before a fall
Egos, negativity, fear of failure, impatience, taking the moral high ground and over-critical judgement all kill the creativity spark and dampen the will of others to question the status quo. All working environments need a freshness to remain alive, and a willingness to listen and learn from others.

A stitch in time saves nine
Don't leave warning and enquiries to the last minute. Although it is a commonly heard belief that pressure deadlines are the master of creativity, research shows that is not the case. Having focused time to create, then reflect and question the theory, brings a greater degree of success into the equation. Be aware of what is going on around you, and use creativity as a means of resolution. Be passionate about what you are doing, so it is a pleasure to know that you are cooperating with others to keep the wheels gliding.

ACTIVE TEAM DYNAMICS
Sustaining creative collaboration. The most difficult aspect is not only sparking creativity in the beginning, but genuinely sustaining it. Working with the team, a manager must be able to inspire the creative spirit and keep it fresh and alive. This means keeping a finger on the pulse of the team and being connected and open-minded with them.

There is a need to have time as a group and individually to be reflective: time to examine the workings within the business, review completed projects, looking for improvements and moving ahead.

Here are some straightforward actions and suggestions to aid you as a manager in the process of active team dynamics – sustaining creative collaboration:

◆ *away days*

◆ *simple creative thinking techniques*

◆ *communication strategies.*

Away days

Whether planning to set the spark of creativity for the first time, taking time out to be reflective or building a regular time to come together and develop relationships within the company, away days, if run well, present the opportunity to bring everyone together to focus.

Secrets to successful away day events are:

◆ The 'away day' is planned ahead so that all participating can arrange cover while they are absent from the office and organise their workloads and responsibilities accordingly.

◆ They take place out of the office environment in different surroundings away from office distractions.

◆ All those taking part know the purpose of the event and are given time to do any research or investigation of ideas from their own team members not participating if necessary.

◆ Everyone attending agrees to actively participate, to be open, honest in their contributions and respectful to each others' ideas.

◆ That everyone understands that, while this event is fun and off-the-wall on occasions, it is for sound business reasons, and everyone will need to take action to capitalise on it once back in the office.

◆ It is fun and relaxed.

Behind every able man, there are always other able men.
Chinese proverb

Away day events are about creative thinking, improvement and moving the business forward. This is not a 'yes boss' situation. As the manager you will need to make sure you are not being overbearing, and that you have created a space that encourages everyone to be a part of the process and that no one faction or character dominates the time. You need the buy-in of the group as a whole in order to make everyone attending accountable and responsible for actions after the event to capture the momentum that a successful away event always creates.

Simple creative thinking techniques

Creative brainstorming
Many brainstorming sessions get bogged down by overriding thoughts that creativity is just another way to look at, or

solve, a problem. The basic assumption is an organisation with a series of problems to be solved. Creativity carries with it the basic assumption that the organisation is organic through its lifecycle. It is constantly evolving, going through different stages of development to be ahead and respond to the marketplace.

Get together and start talking!

Ask questions like:

◆ What would be the ideal outcome?

◆ What is working now?

◆ How can you build on those elements of success?

◆ What is stopping the company from doing that now?

◆ If it has always been done this way – what happens if you do that way?

◆ If budget etc concerns didn't need to be brought into the equation what could you really achieve?

◆ In what ways do the vision and ideas differ when budgetary concerns are reintroduced?

◆ Who gains?

◆ Who wins?

◆ What does it take to get a win-win situation?

◆ Where can you get the support you need to carry it through?

◆ Who else outside your normal sphere do you need to ask?

Perspectives circle

A **Perspectives circle** is an easy and enlightening way to examine the reality of the ideas conjured up in the brainstorming sessions and explore the parameters of any assumptions associated with them.

As the saying goes, 'Two heads are always better than one'. With a group of people gathered together, there is the opportunity to examine the ideas from a number of different perspectives.

Case history

To illustrate the perspective circle in action, a local Scottish team were working to find the best ways forward to integrate the disparate interests of several groups within a community. First, they listed all the differing groups, and having identified them, each team member elected to represent one of them. In this case they ranged from the privately owned property company to local inhabitants whose families had been in the area for generations, the newcomers and overspill from the city, disenfranchised youth, young families, retired members, local government employees, local business, new business and so on.

When using the perspective circle technique in a cross-company creative meeting, the differing groups represented will be the different departments involved. For example, sales and marketing agenda, or wholesale and retail customers needs. Voicing these openly will generate awareness, creativity and innovation.

Having drawn up a list of differing concerns and interests as above, elect one member of the team (the scribe) to write the comments, concerns and ideas as they come out of the session. The rest of the team sit in a circle, each member having chosen a perspective to represent.

Guidelines for the perspectives circle
Have a smaller group of chairs in the centre and choose a minimum of two participants to start off the sharing of views by sitting in the centre and telling their perspectives. Only one person speaks at a time. There is no interruption or cross-talking. When each person has finished, they can move back to the outer circle. The action of moving, physically changing position, is known to be a great way to keep the brain going. As ideas evolve and thoughts are sparked off by others' views keep moving back in to the inner circle to voice the emerging creativity.

Remember, a meeting that allows creativity is non-judgemental and non-punitive. Everyone's idea or view has possibilities – however whacky and off-the-wall it seems. Try the perspective circle – see how it works for you. Recreate your own version and guidelines to work in a way that suits you. Go on – be creative!

Whenever you see a successful business, someone once made a courageous decision.

Peter Drucker

As the ideas and perspectives flow, the scribe is taking the notes. Later the recurring themes, patterns and ideas can be analysed and an action plan drawn up. Keep these notes. They may be useful to refer to in times of reassessment.

Communication strategies

It is a well known fact that people receive information in differing ways. Neuro-Linguistic Programming (NLP) illustrates that there are three main ways: *verbal, visual* and *kinesthetic*. Everyone is usually dominant in one of these types, but we use all three forms at differing levels. There is a roughly equal divide of these three sensory types. To impart your ideas and to tap into all the team's creativity, think of illustrating with words and pictures and ways of *experiencing* your proposal.

Use flip charts to write and draw on. Give every one 'post it' notes to write down their ideas and thoughts then group on the walls to see patterns emerge. Allow people to move around the room if it helps them express themselves and process their thoughts better. This is not to create mayhem, but some people do start to think better or find better solutions by first staring out of the window.

As a manager, you will know whether a member of your team is not taking part in the process or is a reflective character by nature and thinks things through. You will also know who in your team is the person to say the most off-the-wall suggestion that makes everyone laugh, but somehow gets everyone else's creative juices going. So too will you know when someone is being disruptive and upsetting the openness and trust needed.

Time spent as a manager getting to know the teams' individual attitudes and drivers is never wasted.

Cross-company meetings
Have regular cross-company meetings. Arrange for each department to take turns at presenting their current work and schedules. Be open to asking for input and ideas.

Set up and encourage groups across the company, and from all levels, with common interests to meet regularly. Their shared interests and differing experiences can be the catalyst for examining current internal practices, market trends and competitor cooperation on projects. Organising peer groups across industries for cross-pollination of ideas is now regarded as good, exciting, innovative business practice.

The way forward
In order to sustain and expand the spark of creativity there needs to be a two-way communication between the manager and the team. This includes healthy feed-back to the manager and recognition of what works and what does not.

Having learnt about some ways to keep creativity alive, answer the questions below:

◆ What can you do to encourage flourishing creativity as a normal working practice across the company?

◆ Which channels of communication, currently in operation, do not promote creativity and openness in your workplace?

◆ Are there any other ways in which you would like to promote and sustain a creative culture in the workplace?

Now you have your own personal action plan to allow the use of creativity and keep it alive and sustainable in the best possible way for your team.

SUMMARY

◆ Create a working environment that allows creativity at work at all levels of the company.

◆ Make the act of creativity normal in the company to address everyday and 'big picture' concerns.

◆ Schedule in time for reflection and consideration – avoid extreme pressure.

◆ Protect creative time from everyday distractions – i.e. use away days.

◆ Everyone needs to take responsibility and be accountable for their actions.

◆ Assess progress for recalibration if necessary.

Afterword

'*I suppose leadership at one time meant muscles, but today it means getting along with people.*'

Indira Ghandi

So now you've read the book and discovered the techniques for *making management simple*. Let's spend a few minutes pulling the various strands together.

As we suggested in the beginning, making management simple is about *common sense*. It's a blueprint for clear, connected communication and is about demystifying the management process. But above all it is a threefold commitment.

NOTE

Managers must be committed to their company, to their staff and above all to themselves.

The advantages are well documented in the foregoing chapters.

Getting and keeping yourself organised: for example, by being well organised, the manager is not wasteful with their own time, or that of their staff or with the resources of the company.

Being effective: an effective manager earns the respect, loyalty and trust of their staff. They are skilled in their own communication style and workplace relationships. A good manager is ready to accept responsibility and be accountable for their own and others' actions.

Recruiting and selecting the right people: when it comes to recruiting and hiring staff, the simplest way of getting it right is to spend time in preparation. Be clear about the job and what it entails. Consider the skills and personality the right candidate should possess. Don't compromise just to fill the vacancy.

Managing people: this consists of two main areas, delegation and appraisal. The skilled manager knows that it takes time to delegate correctly and allows themself the time frame in which to do it. Short cuts get you nowhere. Successful managers also know that appraisals are a great opportunity which can often be missed. An appraisal used correctly can be a precise and powerful vehicle to change.

Getting the most from people: by adopting a motivational style, the manager always bears in mind the people aspects of everything. They maintain this style of management con-tinuously and keep alert to what motivates others, either positively or negatively. They spend time evaluating what methods work best within their department and ensure that there is a 'fun' aspect to work.

Communication: this chapter dealt with the complex subject of communicating with people, and how best to make it work. After all the most successful managers are those who can get through to their staff and give clear messages. This is not simple. Breakdowns in communication can be costly to the company.

Change management: we simplify the process of change management by encouraging fluency since change occurs constantly in work and personal life. This chapter explains why change is ubiquitous, helps the manager take a positive view and gives guidance as to skills required for facilitating the changes.

Defusing difficulties: highlights problems, challenges or difficult situations which arise from misunderstood communication. This could be perceived negative or defensive behaviour brought about by fear of an attack. Some simple rules include listening, acknowledging, responding with reasoned answers and never making excuses or ignoring the other person's point of view.

Encouraging creativity: in the final chapter, we add creativity to the manager's skill base. Most managers practise some form of creativity while resolving daily issues and possess the courage to reassess current working methods.

If the foregoing chapters have made sense to you and you have acquired some useful strategies for managing in future, you are already a successful manager!

NOTE

Managers today make things happen – and they usually start with themselves.

Remember the four classic functions of management techniques are to plan, organise, lead and control and they form the foundation of most management training. Now isn't that simple?

CONTACT THE AUTHORS

Frances Kay
email: rapportbuilding@aol.com

Helen Guiness
email: contact@fourby4.demon.co.uk

Nicola Stevens
email: ns@proactivecoaching.com

Index